This is Ohio

Geauga County. Parkman Mill

GRACE GOULDER IZANT

This is Ohio

Ohio's 88 Counties in Words and Pictures

THE WORLD PUBLISHING COMPANY

CLEVELAND AND NEW YORK

Library of Congress Catalog Card Number: 52-13241

FIRST EDITION

To

my husband

ROBERT JAMES IZANT

ACKNOWLEDGMENT

So MANY Ohioans have helped me during the years I have been writing about my native state that I cannot list them here, though I should like to do so. Their generous cooperation and patience made possible my series "Ohio Scenes and Citizens," which has appeared for more than ten years in the Sunday Pictorial Magazine of the Cleveland *Plain Dealer*. That series is the basis for this volume of sketches of Ohio's counties. I am indebted for encouragement and editorial advice given me through the years by members of the *Plain Dealer* staff, particularly Paul Bellamy, editor; W. G. Vorpe, Sunday and Feature editor; Philip W. Porter, assistant Sunday editor and columnist; and Robert I. Snajdr, book editor. Florence R. Head, director of the Martha Kinney Cooper Ohioana Library, Columbus, read the manuscript of this book, making corrections and valuable suggestions from her great knowledge of Ohio. I have had unfailing assistance always from the librarians at the Cleveland Public Library, especially from those in the history division: Miss Donna L. Root, Mrs. Arlene Colgrove, Miss Nancy Lybarger and Miss Janet Sanborn; from Miss Rhea McCarty, director of the Ohio Development and Publicity Commission, and her associates; from numerous persons connected with the Ohio State Archaeological and Historical Society Museum, Columbus, and from the directors of practically every county historical society in the state. Finally, I wish to thank Pauline A. Vaughan of Hudson and my daughter, Mary Izant White, who handled innumerable details and without whose aid the text would not have been assembled.

I also want to express my gratitude to the following people and organizations for their kindness in permitting me to use the photographs in this book:

Fischer Studio, Marietta, page 18; Harless W. King, Athens, page 19; Clarence Hudson White, page 21; Tawney Studios, Gallipolis, page 26; Harold Byland, Warren, page 36; Rebman Photo Service, page 47; Geoffrey Landesman, Cleveland, page 49; Robert Hadley, Harry Ferguson, Inc., page 76; U.S. Soil Conservation Service, page 90; Ohio Department of Highways, page 105; Ohio Department of Education, page 113; Norris F. Schneider, page 116; Howard J. Ward, Ohio Department of Natural Resources, page 130; Shaw Color Studio, page 160; Byerly Studio, London, page 165; Wilmington College, page 167; Hathaway Studio, pages 179,

180; Mayfield Studios and Dayton Chamber of Commerce, page 210; Axel Bahnson, page 212; Albert Schroeder, page 220; Swayne Studio, Sidney, page 227; H. Rupert, Kaufman Studio, Delphos, page 231; Toledo Chamber of Commerce, page 247; Edward Solotko of the *Cleveland Plain Dealer*, pages 43, 78; *Cleveland Plain Dealer*, pages 38, 45, 53, 56, 63, 66, 71, 73, 84, 85, 87, 96, 98, 100, 103, 119, 122, 124, 127, 133, 137, 139, 141, 144, 146, 149, 151, 158, 162, 172, 175, 184, 191, 193, 218, 235, 245; Ohio Publicity and Development Commission, 24, 61, 111, 122, 128, 176, 186, 188, 200, 207, 214, 223, 237, 238, 242.

GRACE GOULDER IZANT

Great Elm
Hudson, Ohio
October 18, 1952

CONTENTS AND ILLUSTRATIONS
(*Illustrations in italic*)

INDEX OF COUNTIES

1 The Ohio Company

INTRODUCTION

OHIO WAS born in the Bunch of Grapes Tavern in Boston on a March night in 1786. Western colonization was the conversation topic everywhere along the eastern seaboard and eleven high-minded New Englanders, veterans of the Revolutionary War, gathered over pipes and foaming tankards of ale to organize the Ohio Company. Their purpose was to buy land for settlement in the vast northwest. Two years later, as a result of this meeting, the wilderness that was to become Ohio was opened for settlement, and the first permanent city, Marietta, was founded.

The men had been called to the tavern by Dr. Manasseh Cutler and General Rufus Putnam. Cutler, a Yale graduate, was a minister, physician, scientist and former army chaplain. Putnam was a practical man, an engineer who had built the fort at West Point and had been a member of George Washington's staff. The group decided the company would issue shares of $1,000 each, with total capital not to exceed a million dollars in Continental certificates. Putnam was named company superintendent and from that moment became the "Father of Ohio." The diplomatic and learned Cutler was picked to lobby the company's plans through the Continental Congress. Both were ideally suited to their tasks.

Hitches and difficulties developed. With the Northwest Territory as yet unorganized, no legal or political basis existed to permit colonization within it. The body of laws by which it eventually was governed, the Ordinance of 1787, then was evolving under the direction of Thomas Jefferson. Cutler, as agent of the Ohio Company, had a hand in shaping the document, insisting on provisions for freedom of speech and religion, exclusion of slavery and allocation of lands for schools. The Ordinance finally passed, largely due to Cutler's and the Ohio Company's influence. Application now could be made to Congress for the purchase. But many months more of wirepulling were necessary. The astute Cutler turned the Ohio Company's support to the president of the Continental Congress, General Arthur St. Clair, who wanted to be governor of the Northwest Territory. Cutler also agreed to the Ohio Company joining with another land company, the Scioto Company, likewise seeking western acres. Both moves won favor with the Congress, and the Ohio Company was able to buy a larger tract than otherwise would have been possible. A year after the first gathering at the Boston tavern, the company took title to 1,500,000 acres, which make up today's Washington, Athens and Meigs counties and part of Gallia. The patents were issued by Congress and signed by George Washington.

In December 1787 the first Ohio Company shareholders started by oxcart from Ipswich, Massachusetts. At West Newton, Pennsylvania, then called Sumrill's Ferry, they stopped to build boats. This was about 30 miles above Pittsburgh on the Youghiogheny River, easily accessible to the Ohio River. Shortly they were joined by Putnam and a party of surveyors. By April, they were ready to start on their western expedition. The little flotilla carrying Ohio's first pioneers headed into the Ohio River.

George Washington gave the venture his blessing. "No colony in America was settled under more favorable auspices," he wrote. "I know many of the settlers personally and there never were men better calculated to promote the welfare of a community."

WASHINGTON COUNTY, 1788

Named for George Washington

JARVIS CUTLER was sixteen years old and having the time of his life. He had persuaded his father, the dignified Reverend Manasseh Cutler, to let him come along. The distinguished New Englanders, the "Forty-eight Immortals" Ohio calls them, had been floating down the Ohio River for five days, on their way to found the state of Ohio and to start America's westward migration. General Rufus Putnam was in charge. Jarvis was in the lead boat, the queer-looking one they called *Adventure Galley*, Ohio's *Mayflower*. Its timbered sides and stout roof were designed as protection against possible Indian attack. Behind it came the great flat raft carrying horses, wagons, assorted baggage and men to see that the load did not go overboard. Low in the water rode a string of canoes with more goods, especially food stores to support the colony until crops were grown.

It was cloudy and rainy that April day in 1788. Their destination was Fort Harmar at the mouth of the Muskingum. Mists and fringing sycamores obscured the stockade until the voyagers had slipped beyond it. Jarvis didn't wait while the garrison's soldiers threw out ropes to tow the boats back. He leaped over the deck to the shore and was the first to step within the boundaries of the first permanent settlement in the Northwest Territory.

The founding fathers, after considering such names as Adelphia and Castropolis, decided to christen the place Marietta, honoring France's Queen Marie Antoinette. She had been sympathetic to the American cause in the Revolutionary War of which most of them were veterans. Trees were breaking into bud; robins and bluebirds sang a welcome. Indians were encamped on the river bank and their chief, Captain Pipe, greeted the newcomers cordially. Almost at once the settlers began throwing up a huge bark-covered marque. Under it General Putnam transacted colony business while a stockade, Campus Martius (camp of war), was being constructed. Within this log and picket fortress were blockhouses that served as homes for the colonists.

General Putnam's home has survived and is now within Marietta's modern Campus Martius Museum on the site of the stockade. The primitive house's low-ceilinged, cosy rooms are furnished as they were when Rufus and Persis Putnam lived in them. To step over the worn threshold is to be drawn back through time to the eighteenth-century frontier.

Marietta, the county seat and Ohio's oldest continuing city, with its historic spots marked and mapped, is a mecca for tourists. A spot inaccessible now but of great interest is Blennerhassett Island below Marietta in the Ohio River. Here an Irish aristocrat, Harman Blennerhassett, and his beautiful wife built an elaborate mansion. Theirs was a Garden of Eden existence until Aaron Burr arrived in 1805, the year after his fatal duel with Alexander Hamilton. Burr drew the naïve Blennerhassetts into a treasonable scheme to invade Mexico. The plot was discovered, Burr and the Irishman were arrested, but

Washington County. The Ohio Company's Land Office at Marietta, built in 1788. It was restored in 1900 by the Society of Colonial Dames of Ohio.

Washington County. Interior of Ohio Company's Land Office at Marietta.

both were released for lack of evidence. Ohio militia wrecked the mansion and the Blennerhassetts fled, to be dogged by tragedy and poverty the rest of their days.

Putnam and his band found countless mysterious remains of the Mound Builders. The erudite New Englanders promptly sprinkled the earthworks with Latin names which survive today. Sacra Via, for example, marks what had been an embanked roadway leading to the Muskingum. Landmarks of Marietta's beginning days are at every turn, such as fine old houses and mellow buildings stamped by the touch of their New England builders. The river shoreway is a broad park with a statue by Gutzon Borglum, honoring the city's founders. It marks the place where General Arthur St. Clair was inaugurated governor of the Northwest Territory. Marietta College has fine old buildings and a beautiful campus. It is the outgrowth of Muskingum Academy, begun in 1800, the first institution of higher education in the northwest. Its library is noted for a valuable collection of autographs and Americana, much of it relating to early Ohio.

Proud as Marietta is of its ancient heritage, it is looking more to the future than to the past. This city of 16,000 is in the midst of the expanding industrialism which has been spreading through southern Ohio since the close of World War II. Living patterns on both sides of the Ohio River are changing from the impact of giant plants, nearly fifty of which were listed in 1950 as within the chemical industries group. The development is based on the section's rich natural resources: abundant salt and coal, water power from the Ohio River, electric power from new generator stations in the area and a dependable labor source. Surely Marietta's founding fathers could not have imagined such a future for the Ohio Country.

ATHENS COUNTY, 1805

Named for Athens, Greece

TALK touched many topics during that first meeting of the Ohio Company associates at the Bunch of Grapes Tavern in Boston. Men about to start life anew in the vast western wilderness had a good many matters on their minds. One was education. Out there, in the country no one knew but dreamed about so longingly, there must be a university—like Yale. Ohio University at Athens was conceived that day in 1786, though not chartered until 1804. Not all in the Ohio Company were as soundly schooled as Manasseh Cutler who pled so eloquently for the college in the west, but they were fired with ambition to have education provided for their children. When the Company's plans were completed two townships were set aside along the Hockhocking River, now the Hocking, for a campus and its support.

After the first year's settlement problems had been met, Rufus Putnam, leading citizen of Marietta, and several friends rode north to pick the site for the first college west of the Alleghenies. Selecting a height overlooking the river, they platted a town around it, calling it Athens in faithful devotion to classicism. By the time the county was formed the settlement had six cabins and was made the county seat. The college, originally named American Western University, was renamed Ohio University. It had a hard time, for settlers came slowly into the hills and few could afford higher learning for their children. It opened in 1809 as an academy with three pupils in a two-room cabin. In the 1840s the institution was forced to close temporarily. Manasseh Cutler Hall, built in 1817, is the oldest college building in the northwest. Cutler had drawn up the first curriculum, patterned after Yale's. He and Putnam, for whom another building was named, are regarded as the college founders. The graceful elms lining the old-fashioned brick walk on the green were planted by an early president, William Holmes McGuffey, famed as the author of McGuffey's Readers. To bolster finances campus land was sold off from time to time, forcing the administration to buy some of it back later as the college expanded. It is now co-educational, and state-supported.

An early graduate was big Thomas Ewing, later a prominent pioneer lawyer and United States senator. He grew up in Amesville to the

Athens County. Ohio University's Manasseh Cutler Hall, begun in the early 1800s, is the oldest building in the Northwest Territory devoted to higher education.

north, the son of poor but cultivated Virginians. Getting an education was a struggle, and he earned much of his way by boiling salt. The Ewings and their neighbors deplored their isolation and lack of books. They longed for a community library but had no cash for buying books. However, they hit upon a scheme. All were crack huntsmen and the woods were full of game. One of their number, Sam Brown, was planning to ride back home to Boston on a business trip with Manasseh Cutler. Amesville citizens decided to do a bit of hunting and give the pelts to the travelers who could exchange the skins in the east for books. So Brown and the scholarly Cutler galloped off one day with bear, wolf and 'coon skins dangling from their saddles. They sold the lot to John Jacob Astor, eastern fur trader, and brought back fifty-one books. Young Tom Ewing's ten 'coon skins helped to buy the books that prepared him for entering college at Athens. The library's official designation was the Western Library Association, but everyone called it The Coon Skin Library. The library now reposes in the Ohio State Museum at Columbus.

Long before the days of white settlement, America's first Declaration of Independence was drawn up at the mouth of the Hockhocking. A small stockade, Fort Gower, was built here in 1774 by Lord Dunmore, royal governor of Virginia. He left a handful of soldiers in charge and marched north beyond the future site of Athens on an Indian reconnaissance mission. Somehow the frontier grapevine brought news to the garrison about the speeches in Philadelphia by men like Patrick Henry and George Washington, protesting the British parliament's action in closing Boston's port. The Fort Gower soldiers laboriously wrote out a statement that in the event of further trouble between King and colonists, they would fight on the side of the Americans. The town of Hockingport occupies the fort site today.

MEIGS COUNTY, 1819

*Named for Return Jonathan Meigs, early settler of
Marietta, later Ohio governor*

TERROR TORE like the wind
through Meigs County river towns. "Morgan is coming!" Confederate
General John Morgan, leading a daredevil cavalry band, was on the
loose in July 1863. Galloping into the north he plundered as he
went, seizing horses in their stalls, food and clothing from homes and
whatever loot could be carried off. Ohio's Governor David Tod called
out fifty thousand militia. Federal forces took up the pursuit. But
Morgan eluded them all. Housewives buried silver plate, farmers
stood with guns at pasture gates. Children were kept indoors. And
now Morgan was on his way to Pomeroy! Two infantry companies of
Pomeroy men stationed at Marietta were hurried back by river boat
to defend their town. They got out an old gun kept for Fourth of July
celebrations, laid barricades on the road and hid in the darkness.
Morgan and his men trotted into the trap. His first detachment was
captured, but the main forces went on.

Tied at Pomeroy's wharf when the excitement broke was a clumsy
coal and salt barge, the *Condor*. Her crew dropped the cargo they
were loading, and nosed the side-wheeler into the chase. They stoked
her boilers and forced her faster than she ever had trundled before. An
old gun mounted hurriedly on her bow gave her a fierce look. The
puffing *Condor* caught up with Morgan as he and his men were mill-
ing about on the bank, waiting while one of them tried the ford to
Buffington's Island. The water was too high for a safe crossing. The
Condor looked like a Federal gunboat to the raiders. The Southerners
hesitated. A detachment of Union cavalry came dashing onto the
scene. A few shots, and Morgan surrendered. It was a mild skirmish,
but in it one of Ohio's famous men, sixty-five-year-old Major Dan
McCook of Carrollton, lost his life. And later that night Morgan, with
many of his soldiers, managed to escape and raced on into northern
Ohio until stopped near Lisbon.

Beyond Pomeroy is the Great Bend, the boot-shaped promontory
that the twisting Ohio River makes. Here, near the present village of

Meigs County. Monument to Major Daniel McCook on Buffington Island, site of a skirmish with Confederate general John Morgan.

Letart Falls, George Washington probably beached his canoes in 1770 while on his exploring trip into the Ohio country and the present West Virginia.

Pomeroy, a county seat town of 4,000, was named for a settler, Samuel Pomeroy of Massachusetts. In the early 1800s a coal mine was opened by Nicholas Longworth, versatile and wealthy pioneer of Cincinnati. It was the start of Pomeroy's boom. Today the city is feeling the stepped-up industry generally affecting southern Ohio. Local coal and salt have afforded the city brisk trade since earliest times. With its neighbor, Coalport, it became the coal-shipping center of the area. Ohio river boats depended on Pomeroy coal for their power, and carried it to markets down the Mississippi. Local industries developed from salt by-products and from manufacture of gas and oil well supplies. Hills pushing to the water's edge forced Pomeroy to spread narrowly along the river bank, making it practically a one-street town.

GALLIA COUNTY, 1803

From Gaul, Latin name for France

"Ah! Messieurs! Have you seen this? The paradise in *la belle* Ohio?" Excited Frenchmen passed around a gaily printed pamphlet issued by La Compagnie du Scioto, the Scioto Company with which the Ohio Company had joined forces to help get its land purchase through Congress. The Scioto Company's leaflet described a city, Gallipolis, "city of the French," in the midst of lands with "trees that spontaneously produced sugar; plants that yielded ready-made candles; no frosts, even in winter; no taxes or military service." It was the summer of 1789. France's revolution had started. The Bastille fell and frenzied mobs roamed Paris streets. The far-off Ohio Country appeared as a refuge to Frenchmen aligned with the Bourbon cause and fearful of losing their heads.

Into the company's Paris office streamed goldsmiths, hairdressers, lawyers, doctors, aristocrats and shopkeepers, all clamoring for homesites in the haven across the sea. Beautiful scrolls represented as deeds

Gallia County. Our House at Gallipolis, now a public museum, built in 1819. Originally an inn, it took its name from the host's habit of cordial invitation: "Come up to our house." In it are many relics of the early French settlers.

to those western lands were handed them by the company's Paris agent, Joel Barlow, New England poet. Actually the company could not issue deeds since it did not own the land, having only an option to buy it from Congress—a common speculative scheme of the times. Barlow, who probably intended no fraud, was duped by an associate. The French purchasers' money never reached the Scioto Company, which was therefore unable to pay for the lands and consequently could not take title to them. Further, it was discovered that the 150,000 acres the French had bought were outside the Scioto Company grant anyway, and in the Ohio Company purchase. The whole speculative bubble burst, but not before more than 500 French had sailed in confidence for America. In the meantime Rufus Putnam, unaware of all these complications, was engaged by the Scioto Company to send 40 men from Marietta to build 80 log cabins and a stockade at the Gallipolis site for the expected émigrés.

The French, who arrived in mid-October, held no title to the homes they had purchased, but shelter awaited them. Though disillusioned and worried, they shook out their Paris finery, unwrapped fiddles and held a dance! In 1795 the government as restitution to the émigrés ceded them the French Grant, 24,000 acres in what became Scioto County. But many preferred to stay in Gallipolis, buying their holdings for a second time. The homes they built after the log cabin era remain today. The oldest building, the post office, housed François de Rebecourt, fellow cadet of Napoleon. A brick tavern, "Our House," put up in 1819, is now a museum.

In the 1870s, an Ohio river boat with a crew dead and dying from yellow fever broke down outside Gallipolis' levee. Men with drawn guns had driven it away from other ports along the river. Gallipolis, too, was afraid of it, but two citizens went out to help the stricken vessel. In a few days both were dead, and the dread plague was creeping through the town. Death stalked into the households despite the disinfecting bonfires of coal tar and sulphur burning at every street corner. Gallipolis erected a statue in its square in memory of the dead and the horror ship.

The town's famous son, O. O. McIntyre, writer of the first syndicated newspaper column, is buried on Mound Hill. From his grave is one of Ohio's most magnificent views out over the broad Ohio River to the checkerboard meadows of West Virginia. The $15 million government dam has brought back Ohio River traffic. Gallipolis, the county seat, is enjoying new industrial vigor from the huge plant built in 1952 to produce plastics.

A beloved county institution, Rio Grande College (locally pronounced Rye-o Grande) was founded in 1875 to educate youth in the little isolated communities in the hills.

II The Western Reserve

INTRODUCTION

THE Revolutionary War left the Thirteen Colonies free but shackled with debts. Unity was essential to survival, yet bitter disagreements arose. A main cause of tension was conflicting claims to western lands previously allotted to individual colonies by the English crown. Without benefit of exploration or survey the grants were set forth in ill-defined terms. Holdings of one colony often overlapped another's and boundary lines tangled.

A speculative land fever was brewing. The young states saw a chance to replete empty treasuries from sale of their far-off properties. Wise statesmen, however, realized that the colonies must bury their differences. Finances must be handled on a federal rather than a state basis if a strong republic was to emerge. They urged pooling territorial holdings which then could be handled as public domain for the good of all. After considerable dissension the states agreed to cede to the new United States their vast tracts, with some of the states reserving small portions of their lands to meet special needs. Connecticut's original patent from Charles II in 1662 entitled her to a strip of country about as wide as the state, extending westward to the Pacific Ocean which was then called the "South Sea." Connecticut asked to keep only a small part of this tremendous area as her "Western Reserve" in what became the state of Ohio. It was about 3,800,000 acres, 120 miles long, averaging 50 miles in width, extending from Pennsylvania's western border through today's Erie and Huron counties.

While bounded for the most part on the north by Lake Erie, it took in also the islands north of Sandusky. Except for a half million acres within this Reserve, proceeds from the sale of this land were to go for the support of Connecticut schools, which still benefit. The half-million-acre portion was set aside as a Sufferers' Tract, otherwise called the Firelands, to reimburse Connecticut citizens who had suffered from British coastal raids during the Revolution. This section covers today's Huron and Erie counties and small fractions of adjoining Ottawa and Ashland counties. Within the main body of the Reserve are Ashtabula, Lake, Trumbull, Geauga, Portage, Cuyahoga, Medina and Lorain counties; most of Summit and half of Mahoning.

In the Atlantic states enthusiasm ran high for the new frontier. It was the promised land, offering opportunities for quick wealth. Immigration was halted by the continuing Indian menace until after the Greeneville Treaty of 1795. Then the Connecticut Land Company, representing about fifty citizens, got under way at Hartford. The company purchased the Reserve from Connecticut for $1,200,000 or, roughly, 35 cents an acre. It was a complicated transaction underwritten by bonds and mortgages with little cash involved. Moses Cleaveland, a company director and stockholder, was appointed land agent and chief surveyor.

The westward cavalcade began. Conestoga wagons, hung with crudely lettered signs "To the Ohio Country," rumbled laboriously over blazed trails. Other pioneers traveled in slow-going oxcarts or on horseback. Many walked. Somehow the mountains were crossed and the countless streams forded. When lake ports developed, some settlers came part way by boat. Journeys for all lasted weeks, often months.

Tears of homesickness were dropped for secure civilized ways given up forever. There were jolly gatherings, too, around roadside campfires, lighted as often to ward off wild animals as for warmth. On the terrible roads horses and oxen dropped in their tracks, and wagons broke down. Babies were born en route. Over the trails rode fever and ague, and death. Lonely graves were dug in the silent forests and left unmarked as the cavalcades pushed on. But into the Ohio Country the trek continued. By 1800 the population of the Reserve was 1,300.

Life was hard in that wild country where no white man had lived before. Every item necessary to sustain life had to be fashioned by the newcomers: shelters before they could rest, virgin trees felled and their stumps cleared so crops could be planted. Food was scarce, clothing meager. There were few roads, no neighbors. Worst of all was the loneliness. Families, practically all from New England, kept on coming. So many were from Connecticut that this soon was indeed New Connecticut.

ASHTABULA COUNTY, 1811

Named for Ashtabula River, in Indian tongue, Fish River

GUNFIRE salutes shattered the forest quiet at Conneaut Creek July 4, 1796. Moses Cleaveland with fifty persons, among them young wives and little children, had finally reached the Ohio country. With chains and rods, they were on their way to a point farther west at the mouth of the Cuyahoga. But it was a great achievement to have come this far, and a good omen to have touched Ohio lands on Independence Day. After the gun volleys, they skinned a sapling for a pole, hoisted the flag of the new Republic and proceeded to drink six good toasts to the spot they christened Port Independence. After that they settled down to a feast of salt pork and beans. They rested here for a few days in a rude bark shelter they threw up on the lake shore.

When today's motorist crosses Pennsylvania's border into Ohio on Route 20, he is in Ashtabula County very near this encampment which well might be called the first settlement in the Western Reserve. One family, twenty-nine-year-old James Kingsbury and his wife and three children, decided to rebuild the shelter and remain here instead of moving on toward the future Cleveland. With the coming of winter their food disappeared and game was not to be had. Kingsbury returned to New Hampshire for food. He became ill and was marooned for weeks in an unceasing snowstorm. His horse died. When he got back to Mrs. Kingsbury he found her all but dead from starvation, after the birth of a baby, the first white child born in the Reserve. The baby died later, but Mrs. Kingsbury, though desperately ill for months, recovered.

31

The exact location of this first home in the Reserve has been lost under tangled miles of railroad tracks and a widened harbor. This area and Ashtabula Harbor to the west are booming rail and ship centers for the transfer of iron ore and coal, en route to Warren, Youngstown and Pittsburgh steel mills. These raw materials of modern America are shifted hourly in 10,000-ton lots by giant mechanical unloaders.

Ashtabula, the county's largest city, and Conneaut, both a few miles inland, give little hint to the casual tourist of their harbors' lusty industry. Ashtabula spurted from a population of 5,000 in 1880 to 30,000 in the 1950 census. Many citizens are of Finnish, Swedish and Italian descent and few landmarks recall the Yankee founders.

Ashtabula is linked with Warren, Salem and the Ohio River by a historic highway, now Route 45. Over it pioneers, after disembarking at the lake, moved southward in slow-going covered wagons and on horseback to new homes in the wilderness interior. Later the road was the brisk trade artery for outgoing farm produce and incoming goods from eastern cities. The Civil War's Underground Railroad used it as a main spur for relaying slaves to Lake Erie and freedom in Canada. A hideout stop was Austinburg where the Reserve's first church was organized in 1801. Its first permanent pastor, Reverend Giles Cowles, was secured as the result of a round-trip horseback ride to Connecticut, made by the wife of the village founder, Mrs. Eliphalet Austin. Descendants in Austinburg proudly show you the saddle she used. The minister's daughter Betsy Cowles, Ohio's first feminist, pioneer woman educator and an early graduate of Oberlin College, hid slaves in the Cowles home. She dared to preside at the second woman suffrage meeting in the country, held in 1850 in Salem, Ohio. A unique memorial to her is her study in the Cowles homestead, which remains exactly as she left it at her death in 1876: her letters and pens on her desk, her books, old pictures hanging against fading wallpaper, the same flowery carpet and furniture brought by her parents from Connecticut.

Jefferson, the county seat, is a cultivated New England village of gracious old homes and shady streets, untouched by today's rushing tempo. William Dean Howells, American man of letters, lived here during his youth. It was the home also of the fearless antislavery senators, Joshua R. Giddings and Benjamin P. Wade, Lincoln's friends.

Ashtabula County. The headstone on the grave of Platt R. Spencer, whose style of writing, the Spencerian hand, was adopted throughout America in the latter part of the nineteenth century.

Here Giddings wrote the platform of the first Republican party. The Wade and Giddings homes still stand.

In Geneva a century ago, Platt R. Spencer was developing his swirling Spencerian writing, to be adopted universally by the nation's schools. Robert Ingersoll, "the eloquent agnostic," spent several boyhood years in Ashtabula and Rome where his minister father held pastorates.

Shandy Hall at Unionville, built in 1815 by Colonel Robert Harper, has been preserved with few changes. It is a museum which offers today's Ohioans an excellent opportunity to visit an authentic and delightful pioneer home. Colonel Harper was the son of Alexander Harper who founded Harpersfield in 1798, the first permanent village in the county. The Harpers were an old family who had established another Harpersfield in New York State decades before they moved to Ohio.

TRUMBULL COUNTY, 1800

Named for Governor Jonathan Trumbull of Connecticut

ELEGANT Arthur St. Clair pushed his tricorn hat to the back of his head and pored over the map of the vast Northwest Territory which he governed. On that day in 1800 he was planning the boundaries of a new county in the wilderness. It was a tremendous tract including all of Connecticut's Western Reserve and lands to the south and west as well. St. Clair picked Warren as the county seat and named the new county Trumbull, doubtless to win favorable notice from the distinguished Trumbull family of Connecticut. Warren, in the heart of the Mahoning steel district, is still the county seat and has grown to nearly fifty thousand. But Trumbull County's original borders have shrunk, for many Ohio counties have been carved from it.

Warren in 1800 had two log houses on the banks of the Mahoning. One belonged to Ephraim Quinby who founded the town the year before, naming it for Moses Warren, Connecticut-born surveyor and friend of Moses Cleaveland. From the start Warren forged ahead as

34

the political and business center of the Reserve. Its Mahoning River furnished natural links with Pittsburgh and Ohio River trade. Mills sprang up along the river bank, especially linen factories using flax so extensively planted that it threatened to exhaust the soil.

In the fall of 1801 a horseman clattered into a clearing and swung a small leather pouch from his saddle. It was the first mail delivery in the Reserve. The rider would come every two weeks, he said, riding over from Canfield. Soon after this Thomas Jefferson appointed Warren's first postmaster, General Simon Perkins. He soon was Warren's leading citizen, owning so much land he paid one-seventh of the real estate taxes of the entire state. The Reserve's first newspaper was printed in Warren in 1811, and the next year General Perkins opened Warren's first bank.

The Packard brothers, J. W., and W. D., sons of an early Warren iron man, set up a company for making incandescent lamps and electrical products; this remains a leading industry. The Packards pioneered in automobiles in the early 1900s. When local capital was not forthcoming, they moved to Detroit to manufacture the Packard car.

There were some early blast furnaces and rolling mills but they were small. Warren's present steel era started about 1912 when the Trumbull Steel Company came, through inducements of the Board of Trade. It was the first of those industries that were to tie Warren to the country's steel-making heart, often called the American Ruhr. World War I brought a sudden spurt of mills on the Flats and population tripled. Newcomers largely of European lineage made staunch citizens who worked and fought for America's freedoms. Despite the impact of these foreign cultures, Warren clung to its New England heritages and kept its old-fashioned public square and many pioneer buildings and homes. Past and present meet in the county museum, home of Reserve's first lawyer, John Edwards. It faced virgin forests when built in 1807, and now looks out on railroad yards and factory chimneys.

Not far from Warren in rural back country is Phalanx Mills beside the tumbling falls of Eagle Creek. Its sturdy log dam is still in use though laid nearly 150 years ago by Eli Barnum, relative of circus-man

Trumbull County. Warren's old-time New England public square, the heart of the city, which was the first seat of government of the Western Reserve.

P. T. Barnum. In the mid-nineteenth century 1,500 acres were purchased here by two hundred dreamers. They planned a Utopia where labor and goods would be shared. It was one of several such American "phalanges" inspired by Frenchman Charles Fourier. He never saw the Ohio settlement, which lasted only briefly following disagreements among members over wages and hours. But the mill grinds on, a living picture of yesterday.

Kinsman's early prosperity made possible its distinguished Presbyterian-Congregational Church and homes. They were put up by a master craftsman especially imported from Connecticut in the 1820s. Village founder John Kinsman died early. His capable widow, sister of General Perkins, took over, becoming the Reserve's first businesswoman. Clarence Darrow, brilliant criminal lawyer, was born in 1857 in nearby Farmdale and grew up in Kinsman in the octagon house built by his father, a skilled carpenter.

Niles, busy industrial city within the Mahoning Valley steel orbit,.

had blast furnaces in the early 1800s when household utensils were made from local bog ore. In 1843 William McKinley was born here, the son of a blast furnace operator.

North Bloomfield has one of the Reserve's most stately pioneer homes, built in 1816 by Ephraim Brown, who owned a whole township and carried on his business in a tiny office that still stands at the edge of his farm. At West Farmington was the influential Western Reserve Seminary, its buildings long since razed by fire. Bristolville, with its quaint Connecticut green, was the home of John Kagy, who followed Abolitionist John Brown to Harpers Ferry. In Gustavus the pious Reverend Joseph Badger, the Reserve's first missionary, had a pastorate the latter years of his life. Sent west in 1800 by the Connecticut Missionary Society, he rode forth in fair weather and foul, carrying religion in his saddlebags to practically every corner of the Reserve.

MAHONING COUNTY, 1846

An Indian word meaning "salt lick"

Mrs. Young was homesick, and terrified of the Indians. Reluctantly her husband John agreed to leave the settlement he had platted on the Mahoning and go back to New York State. That was 1803, only a few months before Ohio became a state. Six years before Young had bought his Ohio Township, paying a dollar an acre. No descendant of Mary and John live there today, but their name survives in the teeming city of Youngstown, which is the county seat and capital of one of the world's largest steel-making areas. The Mahoning River's lowlands are solid with blast furnaces and rolling mills, interlaced with railroad tracks. The river over which John Young paddled runs between mountains of ore piled on its banks and is muddied from the steel mills' use of its waters.

Iron in the hills plus coal and limestone brought small forges shortly after Young's departure. Brier Hill Furnaces, named for the family farm, were started by the pioneer iron man, David Tod, later Ohio governor. Youngstown's industrial empire grew phenomenally with the discovery of Lake Superior ore. Ohio Steel, the first steel mill, now part of the United States Steel Corporation, began in the 1890s; at the turn of the century Republic Iron and Steel Company moved in, as well as the locally launched Youngstown Sheet and Tube, now one of the largest local concerns. More mills followed as well as plants fabricating other wares. Brawny men of every nationality, seeking America's promise of freedom and good wages, pushed Youngstown's census toward 200,000. Their homes, crowded into the murky valley, carry no traditions of the old Reserve. Mill Creek Park, scene of early grist mills, saved some of the landscape's early beauty. The city purchased its acres, creating scenic lakes, recreation areas and winding drives. It is one of the country's most beautiful municipal parks.

Struthers, where Stephen Foster spent many boyhood years, was absorbed early within the spreading kingdom of steel.

The east-west line of Western Reserve bisects Mahoning County. In the northern half the New England stamp is apparent in such

Mahoning County. A general store in Petersburg.

towns as Canfield from which Youngstown wrested the county seat. The great Elisha Whittlesey lived in the Greek Revival house still standing in the village. Arriving in the Reserve in 1807 as a poor man, he became a leading lawyer and Whig statesman. He shaped much of northern Ohio's early history. Joshua R. Giddings walked from Jefferson to study law with Whittlesey in his little law office near his Canfield home. His nephew Charles Whittlesey, later a citizen of Cleveland, was a noted geologist and historian.

Sebring, in the county's southern half, has a pottery works. Petersburg, a tiny Ohio village at the Pennsylvania border, was plunged into prominence as the terminus of the Pennsylvania Turnpike and the starting place of Ohio's $300 million Turnpike, begun in 1952, and one of the highlights in the administration of Ohio's only four-term governor, Frank J. Lausche.

LAKE COUNTY, 1840

Smallest county in Ohio, named for Lake Erie on which it borders

AFTER a hard journey from Connecticut, General Ed Paine, militia man of the Revolution, landed where the twisting Grand River finally reaches Lake Erie and built a log cabin on the rich bottom lands. Other settlers followed and clustered about him. Later they moved a few miles south to found Painesville, the county seat. An outpost of culture and wealth, it was enhanced by classic homes and public buildings designed by the gifted Jonathan Goldsmith, a resident until his death in 1847. That year Mount Holyoke graduates started a female academy in Willoughby. From it came Lake Erie College for Women in Painesville.

In Lake County, particularly in Painesville, expanding industry has attracted a citizenry of European extraction. Paine's original lake front farm is the site of the Diamond Alkali plant and the Industrial Rayon Corporation. Nearby Fairport was peopled first by Finns and Hungarians, later by Slovenians and Slovaks, who came to fish and to unload by shovel and muscle, coal and ore from boats to railroad cars.

Their descendants move bigger cargoes from bigger ships by machinery. Patriotic Americans every one, they keep alive Old World heritages with a United Nations Mardi Gras for several days around the Fourth of July. Citizens go about in the costumes of the country to which they trace their ancestry. There are folk dances with performers in native dress. Parades take place as well as a regatta of gay-decked boats in the harbor.

The old Fairport lighthouse no longer blinks its ship warning; it has been transformed into a fine marine museum.

Lake county clings to the lake and was made by it. Its harbor was a gateway for settlers and trade. The Lake-tempered air encouraged fruit-growing and nurseries. Carved from Geauga in 1840, it is the state's smallest county.

An impressive landmark dominating the skyline in Kirtland is the country's first Mormon Temple, begun in 1833. On a snowy day two years before, Mormonism's founder, Joseph Smith, arrived by sleigh. He claimed that in his native New York State, an angel led him to buried golden tablets whose mysterious hieroglyphics commanded him to found a new religion. The community of converts, soon numbering 3,000, prospered until 1838, when it disintegrated from several causes: general panic, the Mormons' bad banking practices and rumors of scandal. Smith fled for his life. The Temple now belongs to the Reorganized Church of Latter Day Saints, a separation from Utah Mormons.

In Mentor, James A. Garfield had an extensive estate, Lawnfield, now a public museum. From here he went to the White House as the twentieth president. Thomas W. Harvey, author of grammars widely used in the 1890s, lived in Painesville. Dan Beard, founder of the Boy Scouts of America, grew up in this city, crediting the out-of-doors of the region with guiding him toward his later work with boys. A majestic old house overlooking the Grand River valley on the edge of Painesville was the home of the first president of the Ohio Woman's Suffrage Association, Frances Jennings Casement, wife of the colorful Civil War hero and co-builder of the Union Pacific Railroad, General J. S. Casement. From the 1860s on, Mrs. Casement was an ardent worker for the franchise for women. She entertained in her home such suffragist leaders as Susan B. Anthony,

Lake County. Old lighthouse at Fairport Harbor, one of the oldest in Ohio. It is now a marine museum.

Elizabeth Cady Stanton, Mary A. Livermore and Lucy Stone. One of Mrs. Casement's young followers was Florence E. Allen of Cleveland, now a distinguished judge who makes her home in Mentor. As one of six judges on the United States Circuit Court of Appeals she is the first woman in the world to sit on a bench of general federal jurisdiction.

GEAUGA COUNTY, 1805

From an Indian word for "raccoon." The Grand River originally was called the Geauga River.

ONE RAW spring day an Indian woman sampled sap oozing from a maple tree and decided to add some of it to her kettle of deer meat. That night she served the meat encrusted in a golden sugary syrup. Word of the new food spread from wigwam to wigwam. White settlers adopted the delicacy. Boiling down the juice of the hard maple became an important American industry in which Ohio ranks third, and Geauga, "the sweetest" county, leads the state. On 500 of Geauga's trim farms a quarter of a million trees are tapped, yielding 60,000 gallons of maple syrup and a $400,000 revenue. Making maple sugar, the main frontier sweet, fell off when cane sugar became plentiful. Today, with a renewed consumer demand for maple products, farmers are taking better care of their maple woods and processing more syrup every year, using modern labor-saving methods. Geauga County stages a gala Maple Festival at season's end, the latter part of March, in Chardon, county seat, and in a pioneer "sugaring-off" in Burton. Two hundred thousand visitors annually attend these festivities.

In Geauga County frontier life was full of hardship. The hills, which add so much beauty, made travel difficult for decades. Forests were heavy, roads impassable. Three rivers, the Chagrin, the Grand and the Cuyahoga, rise in the county. No large cities or large-scale manufacturing developed, the three largest towns being Chardon, Burton and Middlefield. It has remained essentially an agricultural county. There have been some newcomers: wealthy Clevelanders, smaller

Geauga County. Tradition has it that Brigham Young married Mary Ann Angell on the porch of this house at Newbury. She was one of his twenty-seven wives.

homesteaders commuting to Cleveland offices and factories, and of late, numerous Amish. However, many residents are descendants of early settlers. Little white farmhouses, patterned after Connecticut's, dot the rolling land.

An Ohio Cradle of Liberty is Newbury's little white chapel, on Route 44. It was built in 1856 by indignant citizens who donated land, lumber and labor when young James A. Garfield was refused permission to speak in a local church because he was a member of a new denomination, the Disciple Church. Later he dedicated Newbury's little chapel to freedom of speech. Many progressive-minded citizens, outlawed elsewhere as radicals, mounted the chapel rostrum. Among them were temperance and woman suffrage leaders like Susan B. Anthony and the local feminist Ellen Munn who, in a long coat and full trousers, aired her ideas of reform in dress. In 1876, on America's hundredth anniversary, a freedom oak was planted and at its roots were buried records of woman's fight for suffrage.

Towering beside the deep gorge of the Grand River at Parkman is an old mill, originally built in 1806 under the direction of the town founder, Samuel Parkman from Boston. As the only grist mill between Painesville and Warren it was a godsend to the settlers. For the first grinding of 1,000 bushels of wheat, the grain was cleaned by rolling it in precious homespun sheets borrowed from local housewives.

Burton's Geauga County Museum on the village green, a pleasant old house, is the gift of Representative Frances P. Bolton. Burton was the home of Fred J. Gould, famous for his only poem, "Remember the Maine," commemorating the sinking of Dewey's flagship in Havana harbor. Charles M. Hall, inventor of processed aluminum was born in nearby Thompson. The progressive county's zoning laws forbid roadside billboards, and this has preserved scenic charm.

PORTAGE COUNTY, 1807

Named for an Indian trail between the Cuyahoga and Tuscarawas Rivers

THE MIGHTY scout Sam Brady, Ohio's Daniel Boone, had dodged Indians all day. Now they had him cornered at a narrow bend in the crooked river the red men called Cuyahoga. Over his shoulder he could see the savages steadily, stealthily creeping nearer. He had one chance of escape. Flexing his rippling muscles he took it—he leaped to the opposite bank, across twenty-two feet of foaming waters. His pursuers stopped in startled admiration. Brady caught his breath and dashed off to hide in safety under lily pads in a nearby pond, ever after called Brady Lake. "The Leap" took place in Portage County in the heart of today's Kent, decades before county or town was dreamed of. On the heights above the spot sprawls the trim campus of Kent State University. Begun in 1913 as a two-year normal school with a handful of students reciting in tents in unmowed fields, it is now a full-fledged university with an enrollment of over 5,000 and dozens of modern buildings. Many students earn part of their college expenses by working at the revived Ravenna Arsenal, built during World War II and a far different industry from

44

Portage County. In the 1780s the daring scout and Indian hunter Samuel Brady hid in this lake, under a lily pad. Since then the place has been known as Brady's Lake.

Ravenna's principal one of a century ago, a sedate carriage works. Ravenna, the county seat, is a changing city with many dignified old homes as reminders of other days.

Another seat of learning in the county is Hiram College, in the bucolic village of Hiram. The hilltop campus was fashioned from a cornfield a century ago by the Disciple Church, a denomination which flowered in this area. The long list of distinguished graduates includes United States President James A. Garfield, the poet Vachel Lindsay, Educator B. A. Hinsdale, and Hiram's emeritus professor Dr. John Kenyon, compiler of dictionaries and an authority on American pronunciation.

The mellow air of Deerfield, pioneer stronghold of Methodism, is shattered these days by thundering truck traffic following old-time routes used by Indians, cattle drovers and stagecoaches. General Ulysses S. Grant's father and grandmother once lived here. Aurora, one-time cheese center, is a Cleveland commuters' community. Atwater's first citizens laid out wide streets and built a large Congrega-

45

tional Church which is one of Ohio's finest examples of early architecture.

CUYAHOGA COUNTY, 1810

Named for the Cuyahoga River

A LARGE log cabin—with an attic—went up on the Cuyahoga River bank. It was the first house in Cleveland, now Ohio's largest city. Lorenzo Carter began it as soon as he arrived in 1797. Carter was Cleveland's first permanent citizen, a versatile man equipped to meet frontier problems. He selected a location near some crude shelters abandoned the previous year by surveyors under Moses Cleaveland, who platted the place and named it for himself —the spelling was changed later. Though he stayed briefly and never returned, Cleaveland had faith in his town's future, stating that some day he believed it might be as large as Windham, Connecticut, then a village of 2,700. Carter, too, believed in the location and came to stay. His cabin became the center of the settlement, where immigrants were lodged, where the first church service, wedding, and ball were held and the first lawbreaker was jailed. He had a trading post patronized by Indians who paddled to it over the river they called Cuyahoga, meaning "crooked." They beached their craft on the muddy bank from which Carter later launched his thirty-ton Zephyr, the first of many vessels to be built in that harbor. It is the same spot, dredged so much deeper and wider, which today admits the giant, diesel-powered freighters weighted with rust-red ore from the Northwest. The settlement grew slowly. In 1810 the population was fifty-seven. Looking down from an airplane on Greater Cleveland today, we see it stretching thirty miles along Lake Erie's shore, and more than ten miles inland. The low, half-mile-wide valley of the winding Cuyahoga, dividing the city, is filled with warehouses, steel mills, oil refineries and forests of smoke stacks belching their flames skyward.

From all this it is hard to imagine 1825 when Cleveland with a population of 606 and fifty houses was chosen as the terminus of the Ohio Canal, the boost that started the city toward its present status

Cuyahoga County. Cleveland's waterfront. In the background is the Terminal Tower; in the left foreground is the Cleveland Stadium, home of the Cleveland Indians baseball team.

of one of the world's great steel-producing centers. At that time many towns in the Reserve like Ashtabula, Chagrin Falls and Poland were larger and Painesville, for example, was twice Cleveland's size. The first directory, in 1837, recorded a population that was 9,000; 117 million pounds of canal freight worth over $2 million dollars and 2,000 steamboats and sailing vessels using the lake port.

In the 1840s Jeptha H. Wade, a name that was to figure from then on in local annals, set up telegraph poles in the streets, inaugurating service which was the forerunner of Western Union and connecting the city with northern Michigan where iron ore was discovered. By 1850 the first barrels of ore were shipped from those fields into Cleveland, and a blast furnace was going. The opening of the Sault Sainte Marie Canal made the northwest ore easily accessible to the northern Ohio city which was using the good timber at hand to build ships as ore carriers (pigmy vessels compared with today's giant freighters). A 550-ton Cleveland boat was the first to haul ore through "the Soo." In Cleveland the lake-borne ore met rail-borne coal from Pennsylvania. Trade was organized by astute businessmen: the Mathers, Nortons, Oglebays, Browns and Hannas, who built fortunes and family dynasties which were to dominate the city economically and socially for generations. While Captain Alva Bradley's brigs were dumping iron ore on Cleveland's wharves, Alexander Brown invented hoisting machinery to make unloading a far speedier process than by hand shovel and wheelbarrow. Charles Brush, another inventor, flooded Public Square with the brilliant glow of his arclight.

A new industry brought thirty refineries producing "coal oil" and a by-product, gasoline, which was not used. A young man in his twenties, John D. Rockefeller, organized these small refineries, and combined with Stephen V. Harkness and Henry M. Flager in 1870 to begin the Standard Oil Company. Before the turn of the century it had a monopoly of all American oil fields. Rockefeller maintained Forest Hills, a large estate in East Cleveland, and long before his death in 1937 his fortune was estimated at a billion dollars. The valley known as Kingsbury Run, where Rockefeller started, is filled today with refinery domes and oil tanks. A contemporary of young Rockefeller was Mark Hanna, building his empire of coal, ore and shipping. Later, as United States senator, he became a power in Republican politics and mentor of President William McKinley.

Cleveland, busy with commercial matters, did not have a public high school until 1856. Shortly before, Cleveland University was opened on Ontario Street, but had a short life. A club of studious young men, the Arkites, headed by Leonard and William Case, started a natural science museum and a library association, antecedent of Cleveland's nationally famous public library system. In 1880, in the Case home on Rockwell Street, the first of Cleveland's colleges, now Case Institute of Technology, was started. Two years later Western Reserve College moved to the city from Hudson, becoming Western Reserve University. Cleveland's other colleges include Fenn College, a downtown institution connected with the Y.M.C.A. and the John Huntington Polytechnic Institute; John Carroll University, St. John's College and Notre Dame College for Women, Ursuline College, all maintained by the Roman Catholic Church; and Cleveland College, a downtown center of Western Reserve University.

Cleveland had an opera house in the 1870s and by 1915 a successful little theater, the Play House. The Cleveland Symphony Orchestra, organized in 1918, occupies a million-dollar home, Severance Hall. It is located at University Circle, overlooking Wade Park, one of

Cuyahoga County. Industrial scene among the ore docks and steel mills in Cleveland.

Cleveland's beauty spots. Nearby is Cleveland's nationally known Museum of Art, the campus of Western Reserve University and the extensive University Hospital group, Case Institute, the Cleveland Institute of Art and the Western Reserve Historical Society.

Wade, Gordon and Rockefeller parks wind through the city, preserving the names of the donors, while the Metropolitan Park system, a belt of beauty, circles city outskirts. In one city park twenty-three nationalities maintain Cultural Gardens, unique symbols of international brotherhood in free America. Steady streams of Europeans diluted the pioneer Yankee strain, producing a sturdy citizenry with 60 per cent of foreign birth or parentage. Harmonious relations exist with the city's large Negro group which maintains a widely acclaimed cultural center, Karamu Theater. Cleveland's extensive suburbs include Lakewood, a residential district of 69,000 on the west side. Shaker Heights, named for a pioneer Shaker settlement, now a municipality of 30,000, was opened in 1916 by M. J. and O. P. Van Sweringen, the bachelor brothers who re-made Cleveland. They built the city Rapid Transit system and their greatest monument, the Union Terminal Group. Built on the Public Square after 1,400 buildings were razed, it was completed in 1930, at a cost of $179 million. It includes a railroad station area of over three acres, several large office buildings, a hotel and stores. The whole is topped by the 708-foot Terminal Tower, the tallest building west of New York City and Cleveland's dominating landmark. A statute of Surveyor Moses Cleaveland stands in the shadow of the Tower on the ten-acre Public Square he laid out. The year the Terminal Group was dedicated, the Republic Steel Corporation was formed. Its plant in the "Flats," as the Cuyahoga River Valley is known, occupies several hundred acres and is one of the largest single employers in the city.

Cleveland, which recently adopted the slogan "Best Location in the Nation," was well located to supply the metal needs for factories, farms and homes during frontier times. As a result the city grew into a national manufacturing center for precision parts, machine tools and metal screws and bolts. Other large-scale manufacturing includes textiles, clothing, paints, petroleum products, publishing and printing. The annual volume of output in 1952 was estimated at $3 billion, three hundred million.

The early Western Reserve flavor remains in surrounding towns like Chagrin Falls, so named by Cleaveland when he mistook the river here for the Cuyahoga; Brecksville, once a busy stagecoach stop, with many residents traveling daily to business in Cleveland, 15 miles away. At Berea is Baldwin-Wallace College, a consolidation of German Wallace College with one founded by a man who made his fortune in grindstones. In the county adjacent to the city are large glass-covered acres where vegetables are grown, the largest produce hot-houses anywhere except in England. Cleveland, the county seat, dominates all of Cuyahoga County.

SUMMIT COUNTY, 1840

So-named because the highest point along the Ohio canal, Portage Summit, was within its border

ENTHUSIASTICALLY the slight twenty-nine-year-old doctor from New York outlined his ideas for a rubber factory in Akron. Solemn-faced businessmen listened as Benjamin Franklin Goodrich continued: "I'd start with fire hose—rubber would make better hose than leather because it would not burst. Then I'd get into other lines like wringer rolls, fruit jar rings and maybe billiard cues. . . ." At that time, 1870, only small quantities of rubber products, such as raincoats and overshoes, were made in a few not very profitable factories in the east. Goodrich had had some contact with one of these. Unlike his contemporaries who had found few uses for rubber, Goodrich saw great commercial possibilities in the substance. Influenced by what he had heard of Akron as a growing town of progressive wealthy citizens, he picked it as a place to start a factory. Now he was seeking capital. One by one his listeners were won by his belief in the new field. Then and there they made $500 and $1,000 pledges until $13,500 was subscribed. Borrowing more capital, Goodrich opened Akron's first rubber factory.

From such pioneering, Akron was to develop as the rubber center of the globe with 28 rubber corporations, large and small, which were to chalk up over a $2½ billion annual volume of business. Goodyear

Tire and Rubber Company, founded here in 1898, a billion-dollar concern, is the world's largest rubber company. This company, with Goodrich, Firestone Tire and Rubber Company, and the General Tire Company, all located in Akron, are four of the largest rubber companies in existence. Akron supplies more than 75 per cent of the world's rubber needs—everything from pencil erasers to Gargantuan truck tires. The motor vehicle tire output alone equals that of all other rubber products combined. The tire business was fanned to life around 1890 with the bicycle craze which depended on pneumatic tires. It was swept to giant proportions by the automobile age. Today, rubber tires from Akron roll on roads in every country of the earth, and fly the air wherever man takes to wings.

Goodrich did not live to see the boom of rubber's new day. Always plagued by ill health, he died in 1888. But he had turned his factory over to one of his original backers, Colonel George Perkins, who was the grandson of General Simon Perkins, first citizen of Warren. In 1804 the general had paid a little over four dollars for 1,000 acres of what appeared to be worthless land on the site of today's Akron. In 1825 when General Perkins saw that the canal from Cleveland was to go through his property, he rode over from Warren and laid out a town at the first lock. He gave it the Greek name *Akron,* "city on a hill." It became the Summit County seat. Population by 1850 was 3,000, and a hundred years later 275,000. Akron, a backwoods hamlet with no geographical advantages, became one of the country's important cities because of rubber. In World War I, the first war in which rubber was widely used, rubber consumption jumped, and it was used still more in World War II. Rubber companies bought plantations in Liberia, Malay, Sumatra, Brazil, wherever the trees grew which gave the milky rubber sap. World War II in the Pacific cut the supply of natural rubber and forced experiment and development in the miracle world of synthetics and plastics, now so important a division of the industry.

Akron attracted other businesses besides rubber, including what is rated the largest cereal firm in the world. Grain is carried today in pipes beneath Akron's streets from its vast elevators to freight cars. The company, now the Quaker Oats Company, is an outgrowth of one founded by the eccentric German immigrant Ferdinand Schumacher

Summit County. One of the largest ever built, this airplane tire weighs a total of 4,000 pounds and is a product of the Goodyear Tire and Rubber Company, Akron, the largest rubber company in the world.

who invented a process for precooking oatmeal. The city has a fishing tackle business second only to one in Norway. From early days the city has been headquarters for important clay products.

Constantly struggling for space for home and factories, Akron pushed out into surrounding communities like Cuyahoga Falls and Stow. It touched Barberton, founded by the millionaire Match King with the amazing name, Ohio Columbus Barber. By 1881 his fabulous Diamond Match Company was a $6 million monopoly practically controlling a world market. Also pulled into the Akron orbit was the little village of Tallmadge, laid out in 1809 by a Connecticut dreamer, Reverend David Bacon, as a religious community for Congregationalists and Presbyterians. The stately village church, built in 1825, the finest in Ohio of the New England type and the oldest in continuous use, stands serene in the center of the square, with modern traffic swirling around it. Bacon's daughter Delia, born in a log cabin in 1811, became a well known author and lecturer, the friend of leading literary figures like Emerson and Hawthorne. She was the first person to publish a work presenting Sir Francis Bacon (no relation) as the real author of Shakespeare's plays.

Hudson, founded in 1800 by Connecticut pioneers under David Hudson, retains an early New England look with an old-fashioned village green, graceful elms and white colonial houses set amidst well groomed gardens. In 1826 Western Reserve College, "Yale of the West," was established "to train pious youth for the ministry." Following its removal to Cleveland in 1882 as Western Reserve University, its mellow brick buildings and beautiful campus became Western Reserve Academy, today a highly rated secondary school for boys. It was enlarged and enhanced by the generous endowment of a native Hudson son, James W. Ellsworth, father of Lincoln Ellsworth, Arctic explorer.

Hudson and the entire county were plunged into mourning in December 1859 with news of the hanging of Abolitionist John Brown as a traitor for his Harpers Ferry raid. In 1805, at the age of five, he had come to Hudson from Connecticut with his stern and stuttering father, Owen Brown. He lived in the village twenty-one years, longer than he stayed in any other place. The house he built here and other homes of the Brown family are treasured local landmarks. Tradition

54

has it that in his brother Jeremiah's barn in Hudson John stored guns which he later used during his bloody Ossowatamie campaigns in Kansas.

John Brown herded sheep in Akron for Colonel Simon Perkins, son of the general. The Perkins' imposing mansion as well as Brown's home nearby are now public museums, the property of the Summit County Historical Society. John raised sheep also in Richfield where four of his twenty children are buried.

The southern tip of Summit County is outside the boundary of the Western Reserve, and in this part are several towns including Clinton, Greentown and Aultman.

MEDINA COUNTY, 1818

Named for the Arabian city where Mohammed is buried

BEES made history when they swarmed into the yard of A. I. Root, retired jeweler of Medina. He offered a man a dollar to capture them, and as he studied their habits he became so fascinated that he decided to raise a hive or two of bees— for fun. That chance incident in 1865 launched him into the bee business. He invented an extractor for removing honey and special tools for beekeeping. Eventually he became the Honey King of America and Medina the center of the honey industry. Root's sons and grandsons carry on today at the same location, but their output has changed. The first Root was plagued by the wax which he viewed practically as a waste by-product of the honey. His descendants find the wax more valuable than the sweet. They fashion the wax, tons of it, into candles, used principally in Catholic churches where ritual requires tapers of beeswax, purest substance known. Certain special holy day candles are as tall as a man. The Roots' plant, ranking third in the country for processing beeswax, also continues its beekeeper supplies.

If bees made Medina, matches put Wadsworth on the map. One out of every five Wadsworth citizens is a match maker. The Ohio Match Company, located here, is the largest match works under one roof in

Medina County. The village of Le Roy with its white houses and churches resembles New England.

the world and employs 1,600, many of them women. Company-owned pine forests in Idaho supply match lumber with a single tree yielding ten million matches. A million matches are produced hourly by each machine in the plant.

Medina, the county seat, and Wadsworth, at the southern tip of the Western Reserve, are the principal cities, both under 10,000 in population. The county is largely rural with many delightful old-style farmhouses. Early settlers struggled with dense virgin forests where giant trees had to be felled and their stumps removed before fields could be cultivated. Bad roads prevented marketing the rich crops that were harvested until the Ohio Canal in the 1820s brought transportation and prosperity.

Le Roy, village of white houses and steepled churches clustered about a green, is maintained by the strict town-planning of the Ohio Farmers' Insurance Company, which has its headquarters there.

Seville is still the "home of the giants," though the giants, Captain M. V. Bates and his wife, have been sleeping for many years in their large-proportioned tombs in the local cemetery. The couple, both eight feet tall, toured with P.T. Barnum's circus. Retiring to Seville they built a house which was out-sized in all its proportions and furnishings.

Hinckley still cherishes lore about its hunt on Christmas Day, 1818. Farmers, plagued by wild animals making off with their sheep and cattle, massed 600 strong to exterminate the pests. Into a forest clearing the terrified beasts were driven by dogs and hunting horns, and there killed until carcasses were piled man-height high. The Great Hinckley Hunt, described by newspapers everywhere including the London *Times,* became a classic example of Yankee sport.

Lafayette was the home of Russel A. Allger, Civil War general at twenty-nine, governor of Michigan, Secretary of State for McKinley, and in the 1880s a perennial presidential candidate. Edith Thomas, born in Chatham in 1854, was a best-seller poet, often dubbed America's female Keats.

LORAIN COUNTY, 1824

Named for the French province, Lorraine

LIKE wildfire the news spread that pay at the steel plant the newcomer was building would be a dollar and a half a day instead of the usual dollar. The prospect looked particularly good to Lorain's workmen, for most of them had been idle a year, ever since the panic of 1893. Tom L. Johnson, later to become Cleveland's controversial "Golden Rule" mayor, kept his generous wage promises when he opened his plant. He had moved it from Pennsylvania because he liked the look of Lorain and its fine harbor. Up to this time Lorain never had learned quite how to utilize that harbor at the mouth of the Black River. For years the town's name was just that—Mouth of Black River. The settlement stagnated because of two disappointments: the Ohio Canal ignored it, choosing Cleveland instead as the terminus, and the first railroad went south to Elyria. The splendid port was isolated. True, shipbuilding, a major industry today, began as early as 1819 when the sloop *General Huntington* was launched by men whose yards along the Connecticut coast had been destroyed in British raids of the Revolutionary War. There was a mild boom when the city changed its name to Charleston, but it could not keep this, for there was another city so called in Ohio. So it picked Lorain. Prosperity began with the coming of the Cleveland, Lorain and Wheeling Railroad, and later the Nickel Plate. Southern Ohio coal now could be linked with ore from the northwest in the port of Lorain.

Tom Johnson was forty when he came to Lorain with a colorful and successful career already behind him, but he did not stay; broader business and political fields tempted him. He sold out to the United States Steel Company and moved on. The steel company built the National Tube Company, one of the largest seamless steel producers in the country. Lorain developed overnight. Local labor was insufficient and Central Europeans, especially Slovaks, Hungarians, Poles and Italians, rushed in. More came during the job peaks of the two World Wars. Two-thirds of the city's families are supported by the tube company. Others work in the American Shipbuilding Company's drydocks, said to be the largest freshwater shipyards in the world. Here, where little sailing vessels once were built, are cradled mammoth freighters.

Elyria, the county seat, bustles about its old-time square, with modern homes for a growing industrial population lending a new touch to the aristocratic city. A few miles away is Oberlin, a delightful town grown up around distinguished Oberlin College. The school was set in the wilderness in the 1830s with the radical aims of offering education to women as well as men, and to students of every race. The town retains its old-fashioned air despite considerable building after the contemporary manner, including a house by the architect Frank Lloyd Wright. Numerous rural churches, long neglected, have been restored to their original simple lines, through the influence of the college.

In nearby Wellington, which once produced a good share of the nation's cheese, was Archibald M. Willard's home. Here he painted the first of his many versions of the patriotic picture "The Spirit of '76," said to be the country's most widely reproduced canvas. Many of his works hang in the public library which is named for a native son, Myron T. Herrick, Ohio governor and twice Ambassador to

Lorain County. The memorial gate at Oberlin College, erected to the memory of Oberlin graduates killed during the Boxer Rebellion in China where they were resident missionaries.

France. Amherst is the center of large quarries which have supplied stone for important buildings in many parts of the country.

ERIE COUNTY, 1838

Named for the Erie Indians

OUT OF the lake's mists a patch of green appeared. Land at last! The good ship *Griffith,* with the mythical monster—half lion, half eagle—on its prow, nosed into a cove. She was the first sailing vessel on Lake Erie. Two men leaped from her deck, René Robert La Salle and his Jesuit companion, Father Louis Hennepin. They found they had stopped at an island. It was one of twenty dropped across Lake Erie like steppingstones to Canada. This was sometime in the 1670s, when La Salle was probably on his way to explore the Mississippi. No one can be sure, for records are not clear about this period in the explorer's life. But if this persistent tradition -is true, then La Salle was the discoverer of the Lake Erie islands.

Sandusky, seat of Erie County, is the gateway to this island empire, summer playground for millions. The city is gayest in summer when its streets are crowded with visitors bound for island and lake shore resorts. Then its harbor is alive with small pleasure craft, excursion ferries and luxurious yachts. In the melee also are sober giant freighters, commercial fishing trawlers and puffing tugs, for Sandusky is more than a tourist town. Its fine harbor brings the city its industry as well. Long before the white settlers came in 1817, the encircling land arms of the bay made this an important trade center. Ottawa and Erie Indians fished off the shore and paddled into its sheltered waters during Lake Erie storms. On the site of the present city, probably as early as La Salle's time, other French bartered with the Indians. In 1760 an Englishman, George Croghan, set up a trading post, traveling across from another outpost which is now the summer resort of Cedar Point.

Pioneers had every reason to believe the harbor would make their settlement a great shipping port and for a time it did. Lake ships brought in immigrants from Buffalo and carried back Ohio wheat to eastern markets. The wagon caravans which carted the grain to the ships from inland Ohio lined the streets and made brisk business for inns and stores. But Sandusky's interlake shipping declined when the city lost out to Cleveland and Toledo as a terminal of the Ohio Canal.

The lake, however, offered another source of income—fishing. Sandusky made the most of it. Tons of pickerel, herring, whitefish and other varieties are hauled out of Lake Erie by weather-browned fishermen whose fathers and grandfathers followed the same trade. The first wholly Ohio railroad, the Mad River and Lake Erie line, gave the city a trade link with mid-state markets. In the mid-nineteenth century Germans arrived in great numbers, altering the prim New Englandism of the earlier settlement. The new arrivals, finding the region suitable for growing grapes and malt, developed Old-World wineries and breweries. The pure waters of the bay froze solidly in winter and a thriving ice business resulted.

Setbacks came: cholera in 1849 brought sudden death to 400 and drove out half the other residents; prohibition stopped wine- and beer-making; electric refrigeration put an end to natural ice harvesting. However, the plague departed, repeal revived wineries and Sandusky's

60

Erie County. The birthplace of Thomas A. Edison, Milan.

port trade increased. The manufacture of paper, school crayons and chalk became important. Today Sandusky, with its flower-filled public parks and substantial buildings of local limestone, spreads vigorously in a five-mile stretch along the beautiful bay.

On the shore at the eastern edge of the county is Vermilion, so-called from the red clay from which the Ottawas made their war paint. The village sleeps in winter, but in the spring it rouses to hustle out its fishing nets and to welcome vacationers. Huron has some lively dock business but in the main is content to be the home of retired lake captains and the mecca for summer cottagers. Milan, loveliest village in the county, is shrunken and placid since canal days when its mile-long wharf made it one of the world's busiest wheat ports. Electricity's wizard, Thomas A. Edison, was born here in 1847. His modest cottage birthplace is now a national shrine which brings thousands of visitors annually to the village. A wonder and beauty spot which attracts the sightseer is Castalia's Blue Hole, a very deep, circular pond fed by mysterious subterranean waters. Erie County famous include Jay Cooke, Civil War financier; Fred J. Fisher, one of seven brothers who founded the Fisher Body Corporation; Charles Frohman, lost on the *Lusitania,* and his brother Daniel, theatrical managers whose descendants are prominent Sanduskians today.

HURON COUNTY, 1815

From Huron, the French name for the Wyandot tribe

THEIR white sails swelling in the wind, their decks jammed with redcoats, a string of British brigs sailed up the Thames to New London, Connecticut. Shouting and shooting, waving lighted torches, the soldiers swarmed off the boats and dashed through the narrow streets of the prosperous harbor city. Soon the sky was black with smoke from docks, stores and homes put to the flames by the invaders. New London was a shambles. It was 1781 and this was Britain's final raid on coastal cities in reprisal for Connecticut's "wanton insurrection" against His Majesty's Government. Off and on before this for several years the defenseless seaboard settlements had been burned and looted by British ships. Hundreds of Connecticut citizens were homeless and penniless, their businesses gone. It was to reimburse them that the Connecticut legislature set up the Firelands, or Sufferers' Tract in its Western Reserve of Ohio, which has become Huron and Erie counties.

Before the tract could be settled, the Ohio wilderness had to be surveyed, a gigantic undertaking. There were the Indians' land rights to be settled. Finally Almon Ruggles arrived to undertake the survey. He had a difficult time because in the heart of the tract, now a rich agricultural area, was part of the Great Swamp.

An early settler was Platt Benedict who, as a four-year-old boy, had watched with horror while the British destroyed Danbury. When he staked out his claim he named his Ohio town Norwalk for a neighboring Connecticut village that also had been ravaged. Other settlers who followed him likewise named their settlements for despoiled Connecticut towns. So Ohio has its New Haven, Fairfield, New London and Greenwich.

Norwalk became the "capital" of the Firelands, the Huron County seat. It is a bit of transplanted New England. Motorists over Main Street, traffic-choked Route 20, pass the homes the founding families built with Greek Revival doorways, sunburst windows and fluted pillars. Fine old trees and spacious lawns enhance the charm. One

Huron County. Octagon House at Monroeville.

dignified colonial with classic façade was a female seminary. The academy for men was then almost as well known as Harvard or Yale. Pioneer Norwalk was an educational center. Crowded into the Firelands Museum in the business section are fascinating relics of those days. The town has bustling modern interests, too, such as a trucking firm which is said to operate one of the largest fleets of motor freighters in the world.

In Monroeville, named for President Monroe, is one of the octagon houses common to numerous sections of Ohio. The architectural plan was well thought of by Thomas Jefferson and enjoyed a certain vogue a century ago. This house follows the usual octagonal arrangement with odd wedge-shaped rooms fanning from a central stairway which winds to a glassed cupola in the roof.

In the tranquil rural districts towering elms dwarf sedate white farmhouses. Near New London is a 2,000-acre farm made from several smaller farms on which old buildings have been restored along original classic lines. Many villages like North Fairfield and Peru are shrinking into quietude. Their once-busy cheese houses and grist mills are silent, and lake-to-inland stages which in the old days lumbered through their squares have departed forever.

III East Central

INTRODUCTION

THE ten counties in this group sweep from the Pennsylvania border west into central Ohio. It is a rich and varied section with pottery-making stamping Columbiana County; the industrial cities, Canton, Alliance and Massillon in Stark County; the busy manufacturing centers, Mansfield in Richland and Ashland in Ashland County. Wayne and Morrow are known for fertile farm lands, as is Holmes, homeland of the Amish. Knox County's hills are sheeplands while Coshocton and Tuscarawas are replete with traditions of Indian days and early settlement by the Moravians. Within the district are four colleges: Mount Union, Wooster, Ashland and Kenyon.

COLUMBIANA COUNTY, 1803

A name made from Columbus and Anna

JAMES BENNETT, twenty-eight-year-old potter from Staffordshire, England, left a slow-going Ohio River boat at East Liverpool to stretch his legs and look about. His trained eye soon spotted the potters' clay existing in rich deposits. He decided to stay, interested some others, and built the town's first kiln. That was in 1840. Other English china makers followed and forty years later there were 24 potteries. Today this city of 25,000, on a big bend in the Ohio River, dominates the tri-state area of Ohio, Pennsylvania and West Virginia which is the pottery center of America. In one East Liverpool factory alone 1,500,000 dozen pieces of ware are made annually. The figure represents about one-seventh of the output of the region's nearly 50 factories, which employ an estimated 8,000 persons. From the summits of the 700-foot hills to which East Liverpool clings, the view leads out across belching chimneys to bridges spanning the river into West Virginia towns of Newell and Chester. Most of East Liverpool's potteries, cramped for space by Ohio's hills, moved across a few years ago. The largest pottery in the world, Homer Laughlin China Company, originally in East Liverpool, is now in Newell. The one major ceramic firm that remains on the Ohio side, The Hall China Company, turns out as much as all the others did in the old days. Pottery executives and workers for the most part live, shop, bank and hold their union meetings in the East Liverpool district.

Bennett, the first potter, made mugs and teapots which he peddled on foot from a pack on his back, later vending his wares by horse and wagon. Many of those early dishes, now valuable antiques, are in a pottery museum in the Carnegie Library Building. Andrew Carnegie had a real interest in East Liverpool, having visited here frequently as a boy. The museum, one of the most notable in the state, contains examples of all early Ohio-made dishes from the heavy yellow earthenware to the fragile translucent Lotus pieces made by skilled European craftsmen for a brief period in the 1870s.

A familiar sight after the Civil War was a big two-horse dray creaking under the weight of parlor organs and, occasionally, an upright piano. The driver, a slight sensitive man with a stringy mustache, would pull up at a farmhouse, unload an organ and stay to play tune after tune. He usually sang, too, mostly his own songs. He was Will L. Thompson, best known for his hundreds of hymns like *Softly, Tenderly, Jesus is Calling* and *Bringing in the Sheaves,* and songs like *Gathering Shells by the Seashore* and *Come Where the Lilies Bloom.* He probably wrote more music and became more successful financially than any composer of his time.

Compact Lisbon, the county seat, has old houses whose doorways

Columbiana County. Will L. Thompson, composer of hymns and songs in the late nineteenth century.

open onto criss-crossed brick sidewalks. Remnants remain of the winding Sandy-Beaver Canal, begun in 1834, finished in 1848 and abandoned within a few years. Landslides, and the need for a great many tunnels, made this an almost impossible engineering feat. Costs ran into the millions. The canal president was Benjamin Hanna, grandfather of Mark Hanna. Another prominent native was Clement L. Vallandigham, leader of Ohio's Copperheads, known as Peace Democrats during the Civil War, and banished as a traitor into Confederate lines by Lincoln. His house is a historic landmark.

Wellsville dates from a few years after the Revolution. At that time a Pennsylvanian, William Wells, decided his farm land along the river shore would make a good town site. In Wells' home in 1800 Reverend John Callahan organized one of the first Methodist Church groups in Ohio. The fine old houses along Riverside Drive date back to the days before the river front was marred by the present network of railroad tracks.

Salem still calls itself the Quaker City, but Quakers are few and only one meeting house remains. The old Town Hall, razed in 1952, was the scene of many spirited antislavery meetings, addressed by such prominent leaders as William Lloyd Garrison, Wendell Phillips, Frederick Douglass, Lucretia Mott, Elizabeth Cady Stanton and the unlettered but eloquent Negro woman Sojourner Truth.

The most stirring event in county history was the capture in 1863 of the pillaging Confederate general John Morgan. This occurred between Lisbon and East Liverpool at a spot now marked by a monument. Harvey S. Firestone, founder of the Firestone Tire and Rubber Company, Akron, was born on a farm near Columbiana, now expanded into a model farm and public recreation center developed by the Firestones.

STARK COUNTY, 1808

Named for General John Stark of New Hampshire, an officer in the Revolution

WILLIAM McKINLEY of Canton put a red carnation in his buttonhole. It was given him by his friend and Democratic opponent for the United States Senate, Dr. Levi L. Lamborn of Alliance. Wealthy Dr. Lamborn, who was related to

President U. S. Grant, cultivated the flowers, then rarities, in his home conservatory. McKinley won the election. In subsequent campaigns for the governorship of Ohio and the presidency of his country, he invariably wore a red carnation. It became his favorite flower, a good-luck fetish. In 1904, three years after McKinley's death from an assassin's bullet, the Ohio General Assembly voted the scarlet carnation the state flower in his memory. Ever since, on his birthday, January 29, a huge bunch of red carnations is put in the carved hands of his statue before the Capitol in Columbus, and is laid at his tomb in Canton by students from the city's McKinley High School.

Canton, county seat, is the biggest city in the county, and the biggest thing in Canton's history is the fact McKinley chose it as his home. He married Ida Saxton, granddaughter of John Saxton, founder of the paper that is today the Canton Repository. During his presidential front-porch campaign noisy crowds from all parts of the country filled Canton's streets, and later thronged soberly into the city for his funeral at the "McKinley" Methodist Church. Foreign and American tourists by the thousands come annually to visit his mausoleum built by contributions from a million admirers.

The settlers of Canton, largely Pennsylvania Dutch, touched off prosperity early with farm-implement and watch manufacturing. Steel processing plants, including the big Timken Roller Bearing Company, and steel alloy factories boosted wealth and brought population to 117,000 in 1950.

Alliance is still the Carnation City, though smoky and smudged from factories that make it the leader in the manufacture of heavy mill machinery and a big producer of drop forgings. Dr. Lamborn's descendants conduct a floral company, specializing in carnations, where 6,000 of the red variety can be seen blooming at one time. The name Alliance came from the junction of railroads at this point, and the annexation and absorption in the 1880s of two adjoining towns. Mount Union College, begun as an unpretentious Methodist ministerial school, has grown into one of the top colleges of the state. Many runaway slaves were hidden here in homes on the Underground Railway.

Stark County is unique in having three thriving cities within its borders: Canton, Alliance and Massillon. Massillon, with a popula-

Stark County. In a private greenhouse adjoining this house in Alliance, Ohio's state flower, the red carnation, was first grown by Dr. Levi L. Lamborn in the 1870s. The house is now a headquarters for Veterans of Foreign Wars.

tion of 30,000, was named for a French Catholic priest by Mrs. James Duncan, wife of the city's founder. Duncan succeeded in getting the canal routed through his large holdings in the lowlands. The new settlement boomed as a wheat port. With the discovery of coal, other industries came, including iron mills. Massillon absorbed the older settlement Kendal, founded on high ground by the wealthy Nantucket whaler Thomas Rotch. He selected this site for the benefit of his wife's health, and to raise Spanish merino sheep. Rotch arrived behind fast horses in a silver-trimmed carriage, the first seen in frontier Ohio. His flock of 400 sheep, the first in the west, were driven overland by Arvine Wales, whose heirs live in the charming house Rotch built in the 1820s.

Benjamin Fairless, chairman of the board of the United States Steel Corporation, was born Ben Williams at Pigeon Run. He was the son of a Welsh coal miner and took the name of Fairless from relatives who adopted him. He grew up at Justus where he still maintains the Fairless home.

Early and contemporary history has been recorded in a scholarly fashion by the Stark County Historical Society located in the Canton Public Library building, E. T. Heald, secretary.

WAYNE COUNTY, 1812

Named for General Anthony Wayne

GALLOPING homeward after a long day of pastoral calls, a Presbyterian minister rode over an oak knoll high above the little town of Wooster. Suddenly he reined his horse to sit motionless in his saddle. Autumn sunshine whipped the valleys of the Killbuck and Apple Creek into a fury of color, and beyond, the quiet hills crept to the horizon. Here was the very site for the college he had been dreaming of! Reverend James Reed dismounted and dropped to his knees to thank his God for the vision. He persuaded a parishioner to donate some land. Five years later in 1870 the College of Wooster opened one building. The paint was not quite dry enough for the thirty men and four "lady" students to use the classroom seats that first day.

The college gave a cultural atmosphere to Wooster, named for a Revolutionary War general. This busy county seat gathers around its wide square dominated by the courthouse, a building of mixed architectural styles with heroic statuary on its façade.

On the day before Christmas 1847 a recent immigrant, young August Imgard, was homesick for his native Hessian village where he knew everyone was happily preparing for the holiday. He puzzled over the absence of such festivity and dreaded the bleak tomorrow in this strange Ohio. Pulling himself out of the doldrums he decided to arrange his own Christmas like that of the fatherland. He tramped to the woods and cut a pine tree, carrying it into town on his back. He set it up in his brother's home where he was staying. Persuading a local tinsmith to cut a shiny star and his sister-in-law to bake a batch of German Christmas cookies, the boy now trimmed his tree in old-country style. It was the first Christmas tree in Ohio, one of the first in America. The next day the many Germans in Wooster flocked to

Wayne County. Swiss cheese factory at Kidron.

Wayne County. Community sale of livestock at Kidron.

see the tree, so like those they had loved in their homeland. The following year they had their own trees, and the custom spread rapidly. Each Christmas Wooster places a tree at Imgard's grave in the local cemetery in memory of that long-ago event.

Natural fertility plus the influence of the Ohio State Agricultural Experiment Station at Wooster has made Wayne one of the best farming counties in the state. The station, moved here from Columbus in the 1890s, maintains orchards, grain fields and prize cattle as practical examples of good farming techniques. Around Smithville quantities of potatoes are grown, one potato farm covering 1,000 acres. All work is by machinery. At harvest time trucks wait in long lines to carry off the crop to all parts of the country. The traveler through rural Wayne County comes with surprise on Orrville, a compact little manufacturing town dropped in the center of a farming district. Nearby is Kidron, a hamlet in the midst of Amish farm lands. Thousands of persons visit it regularly to attend the Thursday Community Sale. All kinds of stock, farm produce, household wares and odds and ends are auctioned off. More than $3 million is said to change hands in a year's business. Such weekly community sales are numerous in Ohio's agricultural districts and play an important part in the state's economy.

ASHLAND COUNTY, 1846

Named for Henry Clay's Kentucky estate

THE organizers of Ashland County picked Uniontown, founded in 1816, as the county seat and persuaded the town to change its name to Ashland. Ashland flourished with the county business that came to it. Good money was made by wagoners who hauled wool and whisky. Later numerous factories made pumps, paper boxes, grave vaults and rubber sundries.

Ashland College has its campus in the heart of the city. It was started in 1879 by the United Brethren Church and during its first years had a difficult time financially. Long before the college was organized, John Chapman ("Johnny Appleseed") lived on its grounds

Ashland County. A scenic view of the winding Mohican River.

Ashland County. A memorial to Ohio's dead in World War II. Located near Loudonville.

during his periodic visits to Ashland County. A monument to him in Ashland was built under the guidance of William A. Duff, newspaper columnist and Ashland County historian. He persuaded school children to gather the small stones that make it, and to contribute pennies for its construction.

Ohio's Memorial Shrine to its 17,000 World War II dead is near Loudonville in the midst of the scenic Mohican State Forest, a tree preserve of several thousand acres. The Memorial, a chaste and dignified sandstone building, houses a giant ledger in which is written the name of every son and daughter of Ohio who gave his life that we may have freedom a little longer. On 3,500 acres surrounding the shrine 100,000 trees were planted in a reforestation program in honor of the fallen Ohioans. The commemorative park was sponsored by the Ohio Federation of Women's Clubs and backed by appropriations from the state legislature.

The section around Loudonville is one of the most scenic in the state. Little-traveled roads wind beside the beautiful Mohican River and its forks. The streams cut deep valleys between steep hills that are covered with rugged old forests, and everywhere is wild unspoiled country.

Charles F. Kettering, inventor of the automobile self-starter, was born in Loudonville on a farm which he owns and visits frequently.

Jeromeville today appears to be a staid and proper rural village. Long before Ohio was dreamed of as a state it was a Delaware Indian settlement of bark huts and wigwams. The town's name comes from a French trader, Baptiste Jerome, who settled here in frontier times with his Indian wife. There were many Indian villages through here, one of which is Greentown, named for a disgruntled British Tory who fled from his Connecticut home after the Revolution to live with the Delawares.

Hayesville has grown smaller and quieter since the disbanding of its once-famous Vermilion Institute. Only the empty buildings, slowly falling to ruin, remain of this once large school. Founded in 1843, it was one of the many schools important in Ohio before the era of the public high school. On this ghost campus is a watering trough, erected in the center of Main Street as Hayesville's memorial to its Civil War dead. It was moved to the old school ground when horses went out of vogue and the trough became an automobile traffic hazard.

RICHLAND COUNTY, 1813

So-named because of the fertility of its land

ALONG back roads south of Mansfield signs on fenceposts carry the word "Malabar." These are guides for travelers to Richland County's most visited spot, the home of farmer-author Louis Bromfield. Yearly 20,000 come to his 1,000-acre farm in Pleasant Valley, beside beautiful man-made Charles Mill Dam. They seek the formula by which Bromfield's worn-out acres, long brown from broom sedge and briars, have become rich pastures.

At the beginning of World War II Bromfield left France, where he had lived for some time, to settle at Malabar, named for a place in India which he had visited. The Ohio farm is near his birthplace where he started work at fifteen on a Mansfield newspaper. Malabar is run as a practical farm, "out of the earth," paying its way. It's what any farmer can accomplish, insists Farmer Bromfield.

A century before him, another enriched the good earth of this county. John Chapman, better known as "Johnny Appleseed," traveled up and down Ohio, stopping frequently in Richland County to plant apple seeds in stream-side clearings. Fruit was a rarity and his orchards were appreciated. Neither money nor worldly possessions meant anything to him. His clothes were flour and coffee sacks, and his knobby calloused feet usually were bare. He was known to endure the cold and extinguish a fire so that the flying insects it attracted would not burn in the flames. Children and Indians were his friends, and all settlers welcomed him into their homes. Shy and gentle, he was a devout follower of the eighteenth-century Swedish theologian, Emanuel Swedenborg. Chapman had a clear, cultivated voice and liked to stretch out before a pioneer's hearth and read aloud from the Bible or Swedenborgian tracts. These he carried on his head under an inverted saucepan worn like a cap. The pan was protection against the weather, and useful, too, in cooking his simple roadside meals. Toward the end of his life log huts gave way to more elaborate frame dwellings in which he felt less at home. Ohio was becoming too civilized for him and he went on into Indiana where he died in 1845 near Fort Wayne. Little is known about his early life save that he

Richland County. Malabar, Louis Bromfield's farm near Mansfield.

was born about 1774 in Massachusetts. No poorer man ever moved through Ohio, nor one more beloved. Johnny Appleseed is Ohio's great folk character.

Mansfield, city of 44,000, is the county seat, a small city with a big-city air. In the early 1840s when Henry Howe, the Ohio historian, first visited it and its population was only a few thousand, he remarked it had a "city-bred air." It has kept that metropolitan manner. Deep-rooted substantial wealth is evident everywhere. Probably no community of its size has as many millionaires. They live unostentatiously in secluded estates on the edge of the city. A leading industry and the basis of many fortunes is the Ohio Brass Company. A large plant of the Westinghouse Electrical Corporation is here, too. These, with several other factories, make Mansfield one of the state's leading industrial centers.

The city was named for Connecticut-born Colonel Jared Mansfield, an early instructor at West Point. President Thomas Jefferson persuaded him to interrupt his teaching to come to Ohio to correct mistakes in surveys. The colonel described Ohio as "a place of wolves and Indians" and stayed no longer than he had to.

John Sherman, distinguished brother of General William T. Sherman, went from his home in Mansfield to Washington before and after the Civil War. He served several terms in the United States Senate and was a cabinet member under President Hayes.

MORROW COUNTY, 1848

Named for Jeremiah Morrow, Ohio governor 1822–26

A PASTORAL serenity marks Morrow County. Here, 50 miles or so from Columbus, is old-time agricultural country. The largest community is the village of Mount Gilead, the county seat, with a population of 2,400. It takes its name from the mountain in Genesis where Jacob pitched his tent with his brethren and offered sacrifice to the God of Abraham. Somehow, the ancient name seems to suit the place, so content with old ways, so pleasantly withdrawn from today's turmoil. The world, however, rushes into the little town in thundering truck and automobile traffic over Route 42, which winds through the business district. The route is part of the highway which in the 1830s linked Columbus with Sandusky and the lake ports.

For the most part concern is for the wide fields and their valuable crops, though there are some important industries. A long-established factory making pressure pumps stamps its products "Made in Mount Gilead," and these are so widely distributed that the village's name literally is carried around the world. The classic courthouse, one of the few original courthouses still functioning in the state, is in the Greek Revival style. Early settlers did not stop with the courthouse but put up handsome houses as well.

In mild weather, rows of aged men sit the day through on benches in Mount Gilead's public square, an appreciative audience for every happening. Like the patriarchs who lined the walls of Troy, watching the battle between the Greeks and Trojans, they are fascinated spectators of a drama in which they need no longer participate. The men are symbols of life in Morrow County where everyone seems to have plenty of time.

Morrow County. Mount Gilead Square.

Highways lead to placid back country such as the section where lovely Mount Gilead State Park is situated. Hills rise and fall gently, forcing old roads into many turnings. The topography in frontier times made for hardship and isolation, but today's motorist finds the countryside scenic and attractive.

At Alum Creek, once busy center of mills and trade, there remains only Friends' Church, trim and sparkling white. It is successor to a log meeting house erected about 1810 by devout families whose descendants live around here still. As Quaker men and women in those days separated for worship, it had two entrances. This architectural feature is reflected in many of the neighborhood's old houses which have the odd feature of two front doors. The first families came from Peru, New York, and this is Peru Township. During the Civil War era many a runaway slave was hidden and helped toward freedom by members of the congregation. The alum, which gave the creek and settlement its name, seeps from rock along the banks but is no longer used commercially.

Farm lands crowd close to Cardington, the county's second largest town. Except for the heavy out-of-town traffic through it, there is little to recall the busy days when the carding mill operated on Whetstone

Creek. Sheep were raised in great numbers, and the mill did a thriving business.

On many of the county's big barns are remnants of a vanishing art, landscapes by itinerant artists. The specialty of the farm was the theme of the picture: grazing sheep, tall corn or blooded cattle knee-deep in pasture grasses. The painter lived in the farm home and often struck off family portraits after the barn illustration was completed.

KNOX COUNTY, 1808

Named for General Henry Knox, on Washington's staff during the Revolution, and the first Secretary of War

Two horsemen rode slowly along the wilderness ridge above the river. The heavy man was gaitered and frocked in the garb of an Episcopalian bishop. After five miles or so he pulled his horse to a stop. Pointing with his crop to the tree-filled valley dropping below him, he said: "This will do." He was Bishop Philander Chase seeking a site for a theological school where young men of the west could be trained for the Episcopal ministry. For advice he had appealed to his friend Henry Curtis, leading citizen of the rapidly growing town of Mount Vernon. Curtis, as "saddlebag jurist," rode about the county pleading cases in whatever rude log shelters the townships afforded, and knew Knox County from end to end. He led Chase to the untenanted forest areas east of Mount Vernon, and Chase liked the look of it.

In the heart of Knox County is the little village of Gambier, grown around Kenyon College which the bishop founded in 1824. Chase, unable to interest Americans in his dream, went to England to seek funds. He managed to collect $30,000, and returned to buy 4,000 acres of the land Curtis had pointed out to him. Selling half at a profit he was able to lay out an impressive campus. He named the village for Lord Gambier, the college for Lord Kenyon. Buildings also were named for British donors. The famous architect Charles Bulfinch had a hand in the first building, "Old Kenyon," an American Gothic of fortress-like gray stone. When it burned in 1949, alumni and other friends rebuilt it, stone by stone, in faithful replica of the original exterior but with a completely modernized interior. Bexley Hall, the handsome building which houses the Episcopal Divinity School, was named for Lord Bexley, Chancellor of the Exchequer, who had been a devoted friend to Chase. One of the first students was the bishop's nephew, Salmon P. Chase, later Ohio governor, Secretary of the Treasury under Lincoln and Chief Justice.

Mount Vernon was selected by the United States Department of State to represent a model American city for an article in the Russian language magazine *Amerika*, distributed by the department in the U.S.S.R. for several years after World War II. The Ohio city, seat of Knox County, was described as a thriving industrial city of 12,000, surrounded by fertile farming country, the center of sheep raising. Mention was made of the handsome century-old houses and the giant trees arching over residential streets. The city's name comes from its location on a height beside a river called the Vernon in early days and now known by its Indian name, the Kokosing.

Mount Vernon citizens paid little attention to the death in 1904 of a poor but dignified old man who had lived among them for several years. He was the composer of *Dixie*, Dan Emmett, born in a humble little shack on the city's outskirts in 1815. An untrained musician, he nevertheless had a good voice and was a pioneer in Negro minstrelsy, organizing his own black-face troupe. While appearing in New York City in 1859 with the Bryant Minstrels, he was asked to write a new walk-around, or Negro cakewalk, and have it ready for the Monday night opening. All day the previous Sunday Emmett struggled for an inspiration. It was a cold rainy day. He thought longingly of the sunny south, often referred to as Dixie because of the $10 bank note in circulation in Louisiana which French settlers called *dix*, meaning "ten." Emmett finally blurted out to his wife: "I wish I was in Dixie!" His wife countered instantly: "There you have the start of your new song." Emmett went to work and the piece was a hit. It became the song of the South during the Civil War. Emmett, a staunch Unionist, made no effort to claim it, and during his lifetime few knew he had written it.

On a farm between Mount Vernon and Fredericktown Mary Ann Ball was born in 1817, and forty-five years later as America's first

Knox County. Mother Bickerdyke, America's first war nurse.

war nurse she was following the Union armies, caring for the
wounded. Married at thirty-two to a Cincinnatian, Robert Bickerdyke,
she was known to every Union soldier as "Mother Bickerdyke." She
began her nursing career at twenty, helping a Cincinnati doctor during a cholera epidemic, and enlisted as a war nurse after moving to

Illinois. Her accomplishments were phenomenal. Without military status or title and backed by no organization, she cared for the sick and wounded. She risked enemy fire to hunt for overlooked wounded, and at night after a battle her twinkling lantern was seen often as she went about hunting for the fallen.

When the fuel ran out on a bitterly cold January day in a field hospital she had her corpsmen tear down a discarded breastwork of logs for fire. An indignant major arrived, announcing that she was under arrest. She answered, without stopping her ministrations: "All right, I'm under arrest, but don't meddle with me until the weather moderates or a couple of hundred of these sick men will freeze to death and then what a hullabaloo there'll be over the heads of you officers!" With which the major retreated. "Come on, boys, we're going out after eggs and milk and anything else we can find," she would say as she slapped reins over a mule team wagon and went forth to forage on Confederate farms. Once, up against it for food for her Memphis hospital, she announced to doubting officers: "I'm going home to Illinois to get what I want." In less than three weeks she was back with 100 cows and 1,000 chickens she had persuaded Illinois farmers to give her. She called it her "cow and hen" army, and it was the strangest which ever invaded a military reservation.

In the triumphal procession in Washington at war's end, Mother Bickerdyke rode on the old white horse which had carried her over so many battlefields. She won as great applause as her good friend and fellow-Ohioan, General William Tecumseh Sherman. ✓

HOLMES COUNTY, 1825

Named for Major Holmes, killed during the War of 1812

HOLMES COUNTY is a horse-and-buggy land of bearded men and bonneted women, the country of the Amish. They live as their seventeenth-century forefathers did when they broke from the Mennonites to follow the sterner leadership of the Swiss, Jacob Amman, from whom the sect derives its name. The church dictates the pattern of existence including the clothes that must be worn: full-skirted, styleless dresses and sunbonnets for the women; plain homemade suits and broad-brimmed hats for the men who let beards grow after marriage; somber replicas of parents' clothing for the children. Hooks and eyes and pins are used instead of buttons since buttons suggest military uniforms and the Amish are pacifists. Only the barest essentials in material possessions are allowed, and no adornment of person or homes is permitted. The strict Amish consider it wrong to have electric lights, telephones, automobiles, tractors or farm machinery. However, the church allows them to use modern mechanical appliances and to ride in automobiles when hired from non-Amish owners. To keep coming generations to this simple life, the children's education stops after the eighth grade. The Amish have set up parochial schools in a number of districts to avoid conflict with the broader public school curriculum.

Emigrating from their native Germany and Switzerland the sect settled first in rural Pennsylvania, moving in the early 1820s into Ohio, particularly into eastern Holmes and adjoining counties. They are scattered also in other parts of Ohio. City life holds no appeal for them. The big hard-working families, even without modern machinery, are excellent farmers. Their trim white houses, with vine-festooned porches and the distinctive blue or white curtain at each window, add an Old-World touch to the Ohio landscape. Horse-drawn boxlike buggies, on which no rubber tires are allowed, wind over country roads. No church spires cut into the horizon, for a church building is considered worldly. They meet in barns or homes on alternate Sundays. Day-long services (broken by a bountiful midday meal served by the host) are in the German dialect that the Amish use among themselves. Hymn books and the simple ritual are the same as two hundred years ago. There is no paid or professional clergy, ministers and bishops being selected by lot from among the congregations. The Amish were conscientious objectors in both world wars. They refuse public charity and government subsidies and seldom patronize banks or insurance companies. Financial needs and loss by fire are taken care of by neighbors, who contribute not only money but labor when barns and homes are to be rebuilt. The church, which

Holmes County. Amish on their way to a wedding service.

directs all such practical helpfulness, also disciplines disobedient members by "the shun," an unyielding system of social ostracism.

Hitching posts and rows of Amish vehicles usually surround the ornate courthouse, built of Holmes County limestone, at Millersburg, the county seat. The town, of 2,400 population, largest in the county, was named for one of the numerous Pennsylvanians who came here before the Amish.

Grapevines overhang the houses and shade the sidewalks of tiny Winesburg. Germans and Swiss started a Lutheran theological college here in the 1830s. After a bad fire it was moved to Columbus, where it became Capital University. Unwelcome fame came to the village from the book *Winesburg, Ohio* by Sherwood Anderson, who picked the name thinking no such place existed. Winesburg citizens were not pleased with the stories which actually had no connection with their village and probably were inspired by Clyde, Ohio, Anderson's boyhood home. Neighboring Trail, so called for an Indian trail through here, is the home of a family-run factory making sausages after an old German recipe.

Holmes County. Amish women in traditional bonnets and dress.

Killbuck, name of both village and the beautiful stream which cuts through much of the county, was christened for a Delaware chief, once a student at Princeton University. It was the site of "Fort Fizzle," the "Holmes County Rebellion" of Civil War days. Copperheads, or Peace Democrats, who felt Civil War issues were not worth fighting over, stoned a Union recruiting agent and were jailed. Sympathetic fellow-citizens massed in protest. Their ardor "fizzled out" and they quickly disbanded when a force of 400 northern soldiers marched in to settle the disturbance.

Berlin, as its name implies, was founded by Germans and is a trade center for Amish farmers. Near it are numerous cabinet and buggy shops operated by skilled Amish craftsmen.

Farmerstown takes on the air of a gay fair each Tuesday for its big community sale. It attracts thousands, mostly Amish, who come to buy and sell farm produce and livestock, to visit and to eat heartily at the public lunch counters. Such auctions offer sociability and entertainment as well as trade opportunities.

COSHOCTON COUNTY, 1811

Named for an early Indian town

THE LITTLE man in the fringed buckskin suit and coonskin cap unstrapped his Church of England Prayer Book from his saddlebags and proceeded to conduct the service for Christmas Day. His audience was a handful of homesick English and French traders, ringed about by stolid Indians sitting cross-legged before a crackling fire in the council house. This was on the site of present-day Coshocton in 1750. The man was Christopher Gist, and it was the first Protestant Christmas observance within the borders of Ohio.

Gist, a representative of the Ohio Land Company of Virginia in which George Washington and his brothers had leading interests, was traveling about Ohio looking over lands for the company. He kept a careful diary from which some of our earliest knowledge of the state is obtained. At Coshocton, where Gist stayed for some time, Delaware Indians under Little Turtle had a town, Goschachgunk, from which the modern town's name is derived. The spot was easily accessible by water for here the Tuscarawas and Walhonding joined to form the Muskingum that flowed on to the Ohio.

The river and the village Walhonding, "white women" in Indian tongue, were named for Mary Harris, captured as a child by the Indians early in the 1730s. Gist found her living at Coshocton, the respected wife of Chief Eagle Feather. One day the Indian returned from a distant foray bringing back another white captive, a younger woman whom he took as wife, putting aside Mary. The new wife was unhappy and, in a desperate effort to escape, tomahawked the chief and ran off. The Indian's followers captured her at a point in Tuscarawas County, called forever after Newcomerstown for the newcomer. They dragged her back to Coshocton where she was tortured and finally beheaded. Gist was a spectator and records all the horrible details. A huge boulder in the deep gorge of the river, called White Woman's Rock, is near the scene of these happenings according to local tradition.

More than ten years after all this, the stern Swiss Indian fighter,

Coshocton County. White Woman's Rock in the Walhonding River at Coshocton, so called for a white captive who was the wife of an Indian chief.

Colonel Henry Bouquet, marched into Coshocton where he ordered Delawares and Shawnees to meet him and hand over all their white captives. Indians feared him, and tribal leaders from Lake Erie to the Ohio obediently paddled in with more than two hundred white prisoners, eighty of them women and children. Some had lived so long and so contentedly with the Indians they were unwilling to return to their kind. But Bouquet separated them from the red men. Some white prisoners wept bitterly in farewell to the Indians, but others rejoiced at their rescue.

A local tale concerns Louis Philippe, later king of France but then incognito in America because of the French Revolution. Sometime around 1790 he stopped at a tavern at the Forks, run by a tough old trapper known as Uncle Charlie. When the royal guest complained of accommodations and the leathery bear meat stew, Charlie, unaware of his visitor's identity, kicked him out the door. Years later when Louis was crowned king, he liked to relate the incident to American diplomats at his court as an example of backwoods life in the United States.

The old town of Indian times lay along the river front area of today's Coshocton. This city, with a population of 12,000, is the county seat. A number of small industries have developed here including one making calendars and commercial novelties. The unusual Johnson-Humrickhouse Museum in a former schoolhouse contains notable oriental art objects and one of the country's most complete collections relating to American Indian culture. The museum was willed to the city by the bachelor Johnson brothers in memory of the local Humrickhouse family to whom they were related. The Johnsons, natives of Coshocton, made a fortune in New York City real estate as associates of J. P. Morgan. They traveled extensively in the far east gathering the valuable items now in the museum.

The Ohio Canal, coming in the 1830s, did much to open the interior of the county. Roscoe, adjoining Coshocton, was a busy port. The canal winds for many miles through here and is still in an excellent state of preservation. The city was plagued by severe recurring floods until construction of the Mohawk Dam on the Walhonding, a link in the Muskingum Watershed Conservancy flood control program.

TUSCARAWAS COUNTY, 1808

An Indian name; so-called for the river

As a nineteen-year-old boy, John Heckewelder in 1762 tramped the long hazardous way into the Ohio country from Bethlehem, Pennsylvania, headquarters of the Moravian Church. With him was an older man, Frederick Christian Post, on his second journey into the western wilderness. The two were the vanguard of German-speaking Moravian missionaries who were to leave a permanent stamp on the state, especially in Tuscarawas County where today there are a half dozen churches of this denomination. Unlike the other whites of the time, who fought the Indians and grabbed their lands, the Moravians came to serve the red man and to Christianize him. In the broad Tuscarawas River valley, a few miles from present-day New Philadelphia, county seat, the great Moravian David Zeisberger laid out an Indian village in 1772. He called it Schoenbrunn (which in German means "beautiful spring") for the bubbling waters beside it. It was the first town in Ohio. Up went rows of little log and bark cabins and a schoolhouse with backless benches and grease-paper windows—the first schoolhouse in Ohio. More than a hundred Indian children were its scholars; they used textbooks that Zeisberger had translated into Indian dialects. The log church was attended by 400 converted Indians living in the numerous mission posts throughout the valley.

After several peaceful, happy years, cross currents of the Revolutionary War from the British at Detroit and the Americans at Fort Pitt (Pittsburgh) brought tension into the valley. Though the pacifistic Moravians were neutral, Zeisberger realized his colony could not stay clear of the conflict. First demolishing the church to prevent its desecration, he moved his colony in 1781 to lands along Sandusky River. Schoenbrunn was later burned by white marauders and its site forgotten for many years. However, the carefully kept Moravian church records at Bethlehem revealed the details of its layout, and in 1923 the town was reconstructed by the Ohio State Archaeological and Historical Society.

At Gnadenhutten, a few miles away, a tall shaft commemorates

Tuscarawas County. Air view of Lake Piedmont.

a black episode in American history, the massacre in 1782 of ninety Christian Indians. They were the followers of Zeisberger, returned from the north to harvest crops they had left behind. Unfortunately a corps of Virginia militia had arrived at the same time, bent on retaliation against Indians for depredations in the South. The soldiers, feigning friendliness, enticed the innocent and defenseless Indians into several buildings and put men, women and children to death with "gun, scalping knife and tomahawk." Two small boys escaped to bear the horrible tidings to the world. In an effort at compensation, Congress in 1798 allotted 12,000 acres in the Tuscarawas Valley to the Indians, with the Moravians as trustees. Zeisberger and his associates started over again. The second missionary effort, however, was unsuccessful due mainly to the growing tide of white settlers, generally unfriendly toward the Indians. In 1823 the Indians exchanged the rights to the Ohio acres for twice as much land in the far west, and left the valley forever.

Heckewelder for a time was assistant to Post, who the year before had built a rude cabin, the first white man's home in Ohio, on the Tuscarawas River near today's Bolivar. Post was eventually recalled, but Heckewelder had a varied career. He founded the town of Gnadenhutten for white settlement, laying out the wide streets it has today. The largest Ohio Moravian church, the Heckewelder Memorial, is here. On its high belfry each Easter, trombonists greet the dawn with hymns, later leading the congregation to "God's Acre," the Moravian cemetery. At Christmas time, an elaborate "putz," or nativity scene, patterned after their Old-World custom, is erected in the many Moravian homes of the county.

New Philadelphia, with a population of 13,000 in 1950, is headquarters for the Muskingum Watershed Conservancy District, a flood control project begun in the 1930s, involving 18 counties and 8,000 square miles. Ten man-made lakes and more than a dozen dams control the water run-off of eastern and central Ohio, and offer wide recreational areas. Lands around shorelines are given to reforestation and soil conservation as well as to game and wild life preserves. The entire program is managed on a self-financing basis. It is one of the nation's notable conservation projects, and is of inestimable benefit to Ohio.

Both New Philadelphia and its smaller sister city, Dover, were settled by Pennsylvania Germans, and for many years German was the language used in business, schools and churches. Dover, when it was an important collection port on the Ohio and Erie Canal, was known as Canal Dover.

North of Dover is Zoar, an Old-World village named for the Bible town where Lot found refuge. It was established in 1817 by a group of Germans seeking religious freedom, and who called themselves Separatists. Labor and possessions were managed communally. For years the colony prospered, owning at one time over 7,000 acres of rich farm land, and property worth well over a million dollars. Discontent among younger members forced the colonists in 1898 to divide their wealth and abandon the experiment. The village center, landscaped as a Biblical garden, and the so-called King's Palace, home of the eccentric leader Joseph Bimeler, are owned and operated by the Ohio State Archaeological and Historical Society and contain many fascinating Zoar relics.

Throughout the county excellent cheese is produced in small fac-

Tuscarawas County. Replica of a cabin in Schoenbrunn, first village in Ohio.

tories operated by Swiss, many of whom are recent immigrants. Plentiful and superior clay make the twin cities Uhrichsville and Dennison the sewer-pipe center of the Middle West.

Port Washington filled in the canal that gave the town the right to call itself a port. Near it, in what was the first Salem in Ohio (no longer in existence), David Zeisberger was married in 1780, and legend has it that it was here that Longfellow's Evangeline sought her Gabriel.

In rural Gilmore, Denton ("Cy") Young, the great baseball pitcher, was born in 1867. Entering professional baseball in the 1890s, he played in several hundred major league games, winning over 500 of them. In 1904 he attained a goal every pitcher dreams of yet rarely accomplishes. He pitched a "perfect game," allowing no hits, no runs and no opposing batter to reach first base.

IV The Seven Ranges

INTRODUCTION

In 1785 United States Geographer Thomas Hutchins began a survey of lands east of the Ohio River called the Seven Ranges, one of the first governmental surveys to be made. A land office was set up at Fort Steuben, today's Steubenville, but land sales were slow. Congress then realized that land would move faster if, instead of the government trying to sell to individuals, land companies took over the tracts and handled transactions on a large scale. The Seven Ranges, actually a land division rather than a land grant, covered present-day Jefferson, Harrison and Belmont counties, most of Carroll and Monroe counties, and small parts of Washington, Columbiana, Tuscarawas, Guernsey and Noble counties.

CARROLL COUNTY, 1832

Named for Charles Carroll of Carrollton, Maryland, one of the signers of the Declaration of Independence

MARTHA McCOOK found it hard to accept the enlistment of her husband, Dan. After all, he was sixty-three. When his friend Abraham Lincoln called for volunteers after the attack on Fort Sumter, Dan was one of the first to respond. Every one of his eight sons was signing up—even the two youngest—Charles, seventeen, and John, fifteen, students at Kenyon. The oldest son, a naval officer, had died years before while on duty in South America. Martha learned that Dan's brother, Dr. John McCook from Steubenville, and his five sons were going, too. There would be fourteen "Fighting McCooks." Seven became generals. All the others were officers save Charles, who preferred to enlist as a private. No other family before or since has had such a military record.

The McCook house, now a state museum, is a proud old classic structure that dominates the square at Carrollton. Dan built it in the 1840s, so arranging it that part of it served as a warehouse. He had a prosperous business, shipping grain, wool and produce overland to East Liverpool, thence up and down the Ohio River to Pittsburgh and New Orleans markets. The John McCooks and their sons, "The Tribe of John," made frequent visits to "The Tribe of Dan." Echoes of those noisy carefree gatherings seem to linger still in the rooms.

Martha, who resembled Queen Victoria and dressed like her, was fifty-nine when the war started. In every battle some loved one was involved. Again and again word came to her of death and of wounds suffered by members of her family. She lost her husband and three sons in action while a fourth son died of wounds. Charles was the first to go, at the first Battle of Bull Run. The war dragged on. At the end of hostilities her brother-in-law, Dr. John, exhausted from his medical service, died at the headquarters of his son, General Anson G. McCook.

Carroll County had other famous sons. Their pictures compose a Hall of Fame in the office of the Carroll *Journal* and include: John D. Archbold, successor to John D. Rockefeller in the Standard Oil Company; Theodore N. Vail of telegraph and telephone fame; C. H. Carlisle, prominent in Canadian banking circles; F. Scott McBride, one-time head of the American Anti-Saloon League; Clyde Singer, artist; General William Crozier, co-inventor of the Buffington-Crozier gun carriage.

Carrollton is the seat of Carroll County, one of the state's smallest counties. Its rolling hills are being despoiled by strip miners seeking the coal that lies close to the surface. To the south, in wild woodlands that are still beautiful, is man-made Leesville Lake. It is part of the Muskingum Watershed Conservancy District. The dozen big build-

Carroll County. A painting by C. T. Webber of Major Dan McCook of Carrollton and his nine sons. It hangs in the Ohio State Museum at Columbus.

ings, put up in the 1930s by the National Youth Administration, are used throughout the summer for camping conferences by many youth and adult organizations. It is also an ideal spot for a day's outing, and is often used by picnickers.

JEFFERSON COUNTY, 1797

Named for Thomas Jefferson

FIVE impatient stomping horses were hitched to a big wagon ready to start west. Those about to take passage in it were being "weighed in" along with their household goods, paying for themselves and their baggage by the pound. Among the groups clambering aboard was a Welsh family of five. They planned to change at Pittsburgh to a keelboat, and thence float down the Ohio River to their destination, Steubenville. The father, a wool manufacturer, was attracted to Steubenville because at that time, 1813, it was the wool center of the west. One of his children, five-year-old William C. Howells, was destined to become a prominent Ohio newspaper editor and the father of William Dean Howells, leading American man of letters.

At the time of the Howellses' arrival Steubenville was considered a big city with its 2,000 population. It has grown to 40,000 and has changed from wool- to steel-making. It dates from 1786 when a stockade was erected to protect government lands opening for settlement. The fort was named Steuben for the Prussian nobleman Baron Wilhelm von Steuben, who drilled the Continental Army at Valley Forge.

The hills climb steeply from the river. From their heights one looks out over the broad Ohio into the West Virginia panhandle and the big Weirton Steel Company plant, tied closely to Steubenville's economy. The main employer in the city proper is the Wheeling Steel Corporation; its local mills are known as the Steubenville Works.

The wool manufacture which preceded steel was stimulated by Bezaleel Wells who officially founded the town in 1797. He introduced merino sheep, which started the early wool-making. The amazing man had his finger in all other undertakings such as coal mining and glass-making. From such industries and the brisk river commerce his city prospered, and by 1827, when Henry Clay visited it, it was the third largest town in Ohio. Clay, shrewd politician that he was, wore a suit of "Steubenville wool" in deference to the town's pride in its wool business.

In front of the ornate courthouse is the statue of Steubenville's famous son, Edward M. Stanton, Secretary of War under Lincoln, and buried in Union Cemetery. George Washington stopped on the shore at Mingo Junction near Steubenville, when inspecting lands his brothers owned in the Ohio Country, which he envisioned as a land of great promise.

At Mount Pleasant where the population is a scant 800 is the second largest Friends' meeting house in the country. It is now state-owned. It was built in 1814 to seat 3,000. Quakers streaming into this part of Ohio thought Mount Pleasant would grow into a big city and become the center of their faith. It was a busy place for a few years, but immigrants moving west over the National Road to the south by-passed it. Though unused for years, the structure remained sound. Girders spread 60 feet without a splice. An ingeniously designed wooden partition can be lowered to divide the enormous auditorium

97

into two halls and, when not in use, can be folded out of sight around a wooden axle in the attic.

Adjoining the grounds is Albi Cottage, now a private residence, which was the nineteenth-century home of a Quaker miss, Abbie Flanner. She carried on a romantic correspondence with the popular poet Fitz-Greene Halleck. A dashing bachelor and member of the New York City literati, Halleck was captivated by the letters, mostly in verse, of the girl from the Ohio backwoods. Though the two had never met, he determined, finally, to come west and marry her. Abbie, however, rejected him. Tradition says it was because she was not pretty and feared he would find her less desirable face to face than in her letters.

Mount Pleasant was opposed to slavery and operated a Free Labor Store, a station on the Underground Railroad, and published two abolition papers. One, the *Philanthropist,* was the first such publication.

Large mulberry orchards were cultivated here for silkworms, and for a time silk was made in quantity.

Jefferson County. Interior of the Quaker Meeting House at Mount Pleasant, showing half its vast auditorium. What appears to be a wall (right) actually is a movable partition that is wound up and down on a giant wooden wheel in the attic. All woodwork is handmade. The Meeting House, built in 1814, has not been used since 1917. It has a seating capacity of 3,000 and is now preserved by the state as a relic of early Ohio.

HARRISON COUNTY, 1813

Named for General William Henry Harrison

"WE'LL pay you $75,000, hard cash, for your place." The farmer listened to the coal company's representative and was impressed in spite of himself. He hated to give up his 160 acres of good dairy land. It was his birthplace. His father and uncle had tilled it before him. Last year he netted $7,000. But $75,000! That was something else. No more work. No more worry. He sold out.

Now the green meadows where his prized herds grazed are hills of arid land. Giant steam shovels scooped out the coal and left the scourged earth in hills of desolation where nothing, not even weeds, will grow for generations. The trim white homestead with its dooryard flower gardens and the big barns were in the path of the bulldozer and disappeared.

This is the story of most of Harrison County today. Venerable little Cadiz, the county seat, is all but inundated by the great waste that creeps nearer and nearer, reaching its hungry fingers for the coal that lies so close to the surface. Laws have been passed aimed at reclamation, but they will not replace the giant trees that have already been uprooted like matchsticks. Laws will not bring back fertility to spoiled banks or stop the erosion on bald peaks. Coal operators have planted some tiny trees that are struggling valiantly for a toehold. But the Great Ohio Desert remains—and grows. It is spreading into surrounding counties, until as many as twenty are involved in this panorama of destruction.

Coal is an industrial necessity. When it is shallow-buried, as in the Harrison County fields, it can be "stripped," a far cheaper process than when dug from deep mines. Keeping down the price of coal aids everyone. Landowners are paid well for their holdings. Many are glad to sell. In reply to all these arguments, one must ask, "What of Ohio?" In this day of emphasis on conservation, is one-fourth of the state to be transformed into bleak ridges and untenanted, sharp-cut valleys?

Cadiz was platted in 1803 at the junction of the much traveled

Harrison County. The effects of strip mining in Harrison and adjoining counties.

roads from Pittsburgh and Virginia. The location brought quick growth, and development of a nationally important wool business. Surrounding hills, now so barren, were dotted with sheep, more sheep in 1880 per square mile than in any other county of the state.

New Rumley, north of Cadiz, is a serene little hamlet high in the Harrison County hills. It is difficult to think of it as the birthplace of George Armstrong Custer, tempestuous and colorful military hero. His modest home has been allowed to fall in ruins. Beside its foundation Ohio has put up a statue to this man who at seventeen left the village for West Point. Six years later he was the youngest general in the Civil War. He stands there, caught forever in bronze, in swagger pose with sword, campaign hat, caped uniform—and long curls. It is the way he looked, one feels, when he was killed at thirty-nine in the Battle of the Little Big Horn in Montana. Custer and his entire company of 200 were wiped out by the Indians under Sitting Bull in the red man's last stand against the whites. Hundreds seek the road to the out-of-the-way village, for Custer lore is growing. Among the many biographies are several by his widow, who spent the fifty-seven years she survived him in extolling him and countering the criticism that overshadowed his Montana campaign.

Two large lakes, part of the Muskingum Watershed Conservancy District, the Clendening and Tappan Reservoirs, are in the eastern part of the county. In addition to their practical flood control purpose, they add much beauty to this part of the county and are recreation centers for campers, fishermen and picnickers.

BELMONT COUNTY, 1801

*From an anglicization of French words meaning
"beautiful mountain," referring to the hills of the county*

A QUAKER youth, apprenticed to a Wheeling harness maker, stood at the door of the shop, awl in hand. He had stopped work to watch a band of Negroes, chained together, trudge over the cobblestone street. Benjamin Lundy was very deaf, but he caught the wail of the slaves. A few years later, in 1815, while making saddles in St. Clairsville, he organized America's first abolition group, the Union Humane Society. He started with six members, but soon there were five hundred. Lundy printed an abolition paper, *The Genius for Universal Emancipation.* He moved about the country from Missouri to New England, continuing his paper, preaching freedom for the slaves. Though always frail, he usually walked. Mobs threatened him many times. In 1828 in Boston, William Lloyd Garrison fell under his spell and became his assistant editor. Lundy died in 1839, but Garrison carried on.

St. Clairsville, the county seat and headquarters for several strip mining companies, is in the heart of Ohio's coal lands. The county was settled early by members of the Society of Friends. Their descendants follow the old pattern of life on their hillside farms and little villages. The "plain dress," seldom seen now among the sect, is in vogue: broad-brimmed hats and oddly cut suits for the men; full-skirted dresses, bonnets and shawls for the women. First Day (Sunday) and Fourth Day (Wednesday) worship is held in little white meeting houses on country roads. Barnesville has Ohio's only co-educational boarding school on a high school level, Friends Boarding School, established in the early days. At the entrance to its 190-acre farm campus old Stillwater Meeting House stands like a spiritual guardian. The pupils manage much of the farm and campus work along with their studies.

The architect of America's first navy lies in a neglected cemetery at Colerain northeast of St. Clairsville. The plain headstone reads simply: "Josiah Fox, died 1847." The country's first six ships, the *Constitution* among them, were commissioned by Congress in 1794 to fight the Barbary pirates. Certain radical features marked a new era in fighting frigates. The innovations are considered to have been the creation of Fox, though history generally credits the contractor, Joshua Humphreys, whose name was signed to the plans. Fox, who had a shipyard in Philadelphia and later in Wheeling, spent years trying to obtain the recognition due him from the government. About 1812, disgruntled and bitter, he bought a large tract in Ohio among his fellow-Quakers and built a house, a replica of his native Cornwall home, big enough for his eleven children. Names of Fox children and grandchildren and their early dates are scratched on several windowpanes of ripply glass brought in covered wagons from the east. Near Fox's grave is the small meeting house, falling now to ruin, where he worshipped in defiance of clerks and overseers. They found him not "acceptable" because he had married "outside of meeting" and had mounted guns on his boats, contrary to pacifist Quaker principles. Fox countered that his "dear wife Anna" was "an honor to any group" though not born a Friend, and the guns were a subject for his own conscience.

Martin's Ferry, which is not far away, was settled by two Martins, father and son, who ferried cattle and farm products across the Ohio River. Its two most distinguished citizens were William Dean Howells, born in 1837 in a cottage where the railroad tracks now lie, and Betty Zane, younger sister of Ebenezer Zane. Betty grew up around Fort Henry, across the river, but later lived on the Ohio side. While a girl in her teens she saved the fort during a prolonged siege by Indians. When ammunition was dangerously low, she dashed from her father's

Belmont County. Members of the Society of Friends at worship in a country Meeting House.

house with powder in a tablecloth tied around her waist. Not once but several times she ran back and forth while Indian bullets whizzed about her. School children of Martin's Ferry collected pennies and built a monument to this frontier heroine.

Over the door of a weathered Victorian house in Bellaire is the sculptured profile of a mule. Jacob Heatherington used a mule named Jack in coal mining operations. When Heatherington made a fortune from the business, he claimed the animal had helped him. So he said his big home was "the house that Jack built," and put the mule's portrait at the entrance.

South of Bellaire, at Shadyside, an expanded Kaiser-Frazer corporation plant started work in 1952 on a $3 million contract for a classified military weapon. At another river location near Powhatan Point, one of the most modern deep coal mines in the world was developed in 1951. Such activities are part of the growing industrialism along the Ohio River from Belmont County to Cincinnati. It is a new frontier for industry, rapidly transforming the Ohio Valley into an American Ruhr.

MONROE COUNTY, 1815

Named for James Monroe

EVERYTHING seemed serene that day in the Wetzel cabin. But young Lewis knew his father was uneasy for rumors had come that the Indians were gathering. The family was admiring the new paper window, freshly greased with bear fat. Without warning hideous yells sounded in the yard, and a dozen Indians swarmed inside the cabin. Spilling out the hearth's blazing logs they set fire to the cabin and tomahawked the father. One of the savages grabbed Lewis and his younger brother and dashed off with them through the forest. The next night, while the exhausted Indians snored in sleep, the boys crept back to their. family clearing. Blackened logs, still smoking, showed where the home had been. There was no sign of their parents or the other children. Lewis then and there vowed that for the rest of his life he would kill every Indian he met. This was 1777, and for the next fifty years he kept his pledge. After the massacre he attached himself to the Fort Henry garrison at Wheeling near his home. He was only a boy, but he knew the country on both sides of the river and the soldiers came to depend on him for scouting. He spent much time in Monroe and Belmont Counties. He was a tall startling-looking man with black hair reaching to his knees. Fleet as a deer and a crack shot, he acquired the valuable trick of loading his musket as he ran. The Indians had a name for him, Gun-Always-Loaded, and lived in terror of him. He made it a practice to spare Indian women and children, but a male he shot on sight.

In 1785 General Josiah Harmar, commander of Fort Harmar where Marietta now is, was seeking peace with the Indians and ordered whites to stop killing red men. Wetzel ignored the proclamation and was arrested. At his trial, instead of defending himself against the charge, he boasted he had killed 100 savages. He was sentenced to die, but Harmar released him; he realized that Wetzel was the frontier's hero and his execution would not be countenanced. The scout returned to his home grounds near Wheeling to celebrate. On the way he met four Indians and killed three of them.

As the Ohio country filled with settlers and Indians became fewer,

Monroe County. The "Switzerland of Ohio."

Wetzel moved on west, and there he died. Wetzel is one of Ohio's great legendary figures, and every county along the Ohio cherishes special Wetzel lore.

Ten Swiss families were crowded together on a flatboat as it pushed against the Ohio River current. Finally they were able to land, at the mouth of Captina Creek. This first band of Swiss arrived in 1819. The hills reminded them of their homeland, and they wrote back urging relatives and friends to join them. Monroe County soon became a "Little Switzerland." Land was cheap as the government was eager to sell the acres in the Seven Ranges. The newcomers brought the crafts of their forefathers. They produced good Swiss cheese, made intricate watches and clocks. Cheese is still made by their descendants in small factories, but watch-making is a trade of the past.

Woodsfield, the county seat with 2,500 population, was laid out in 1814 by Archibald Wood. Woodsfield at one time was connected with the outside world by the now extinct Bellaire, Zanesville and Western Railroad. The roadbed followed so many turns and trestles that it was called facetiously the "Bent, Zigzag and Wobbly" railway. In the entire county today there are only 2.13 miles of railroad.

Oil and gas brought a boom in the 1890s that subsided as the wells ran out. Some, however, have been revived, and are bringing in revenue again. Coal is plentiful and one of Ohio's largest mines is in the county. These industries attracted many Slavs and Italians who are augmenting the original Swiss. Many areas are still as undeveloped as in pioneer times, and scenery is breathtaking.

V Central

INTRODUCTION

THE counties in the Central group fan out from Franklin in the center of Ohio where the state capital, Columbus, is located. Colorful folk tales cling to Guernsey County hills, and old river ways linger in the valley of the majestic Muskingum. The scenic country through which the Hocking River passes has been opened as a vast state park. Newark, on the Licking River, is a city with expanding industrial life. Two other busy cities, Lancaster and Zanesville founded by road builder Ebenezer Zane, were first linked by his Trace, Ohio's first highway. Delaware, in the heart of Ohio, is proud of its Ohio Wesleyan University while Noble, to the east of this division, has the distinction of being Ohio's youngest county.

The building of both the National Road and the Ohio Canal played a major role in Ohio's history. In the middle 1800s nearly 1,000 miles of main canal lines criss-crossed the state. The cost, $16 million, was staggering to a frontier economy, but it paid off. Ohio's population jumped from 580,000 in 1820 to three times that in 1840. Towns were born, and sustaining local industries appeared which continue to thrive today.

GUERNSEY COUNTY, 1810

*Named for the English Channel Island which was the
home of some of the first settlers*

THE perfume of pennyroyal hung
in the air of early Guernsey County. In hilly farm yards, bark-thatched
stills steamed out the pungent oil from the blue-flowered herb. Pennyroyal, at home in newly cleared slopes, spread like a carpet over much
of the land. Pioneers, forced to handle their own doctoring, depended
on the extract as a remedy for stomach troubles and colds, and as a
counter-irritant for sprains and aches. Fields of peppermint, too, were
cultivated as an important frontier medicine. The stills long since
have disappeared, and pennyroyal and peppermint survive only as
weeds in barnyards. But at Fairview, heart of ancient pennyroyaldom,
descendants of old-time distillers hold family reunions each autumn,
the harvest season of the crop.

Cambridge, county seat of 15,000, was laid out in 1806 and named
for Cambridge, Maryland, home of its founders. The National Road
brought importance to Cambridge when reached there twenty years
later. Coal has been an important product for decades, with extensive
strip mining carried on in the county today. Leading Cambridge industries are a glass factory specializing in hand-blown glass, and a
pottery making dinnerware. The Cambridge State Hospital, caring
for 2,800 patients, was originally built as a hospital for wounded veterans of World War II.

The National Road in this county was forced over curious stone
bridges shaped like the letter S. They have always been traffic hazards
but they are so sturdily constructed that many have been allowed to
stand with modern roads detoured around them. There are many
theories but no good explanation of the design of these unique relics.
The Road's stage and wagon trade was served by many inns in the
county including two at Old Washington. In this village the northern-
most battle of the Civil War was fought between Union soldiers and
Confederate General John Morgan's raiders.

At a camp meeting near Salesville in the Leatherwood Valley, a
voice from the rear of the log chapel suddenly boomed out: "I am

Guernsey County. An "S" bridge, common in the county.

God." A tall stranger in fashionable broadcloth and stovepipe hat strode up the aisle. John Dylks was his earthly name, he said. He soon had many converts who built a separate log church. The isolated little community of the 1820s was torn apart over Dylks. Some worshipped, some reviled him. He was arrested for impersonating God, but freed when a circuit judge could find no statute forbidding a man to call himself God if he wished. Dylks disappeared while walking with two disciples to Philadelphia. The story formed the basis of a novel, *The Leatherwood God,* by William Dean Howells.

NOBLE COUNTY, 1851

Named for James Noble, early settler

In 1814 when Jo Caldwell was sixteen, he helped drill a salt well. As the pole was pushed down, an oily greenish substance oozed up to the surface. It seemed worthless stuff to the men who were after salt, then precious and scarce. They had drilled what was probably Ohio's first oil well. When Jo was much older, in 1857, he platted a town along Duck Creek and gave it his name. The county had been formed six years before, the last to be organized in the state. Caldwell, today a village of 1,800, became the county seat.

Pioneers continued to drill for salt and to get oil instead. It floated to the top of the brine, and was siphoned off and thrown away. After that the water could be evaporated for its salt content. Sometimes the oil was sopped up in rags that were then squeezed and the liquid bottled to be hawked as Seneca Oil, good for colds, cuts and aches.

In the 1850s, E. L. Drake, Pennsylvania's pioneer oil man, sent representatives to investigate Ohio oil finds. As a result oil for a time assumed new value and drilling went on all around Caldwell. Some wells gushed up in such quantity that often there were not enough barrels at hand to catch the flow. But saltmaking remained the main occupation for years. In order to market the product it had to be carted to McConnelsville on the Muskingum. The road lay over what is today's Route 76, a scenic highway. In those days it was a narrow

Noble County. Lake Seneca in the Muskingum Conservancy District lies mostly in Noble, with part in adjoining Guernsey County.

tortuous trail with mud and ruts that bogged wagons to a standstill.

A real oil boom came after the Civil War, bringing the most excitement the county has known. Speculators flocked in, buying well rights from all who would sell. Farm pastures which had had no takers for $50 an acre sold for $1,000 and more. The oil promotion soon collapsed, and as there was no longer a market for salt, Noble County went back to farming. During the two world wars another of the locality's underground treasures, coal, was the basis for a new industry. Newcomers of European extraction moved in, attracted by the wages offered in the mines. Today they mingle with descendants of the pioneers, who were largely of New England stock from the section around Marietta.

A storm with piercing lightning and tearing winds whipped over the county one September afternoon in 1925. Citizens of the village of Ava noticed an enormous dirigible, the *Shenandoah*, pitching about in the clouds overhead. As they looked on in horror, the ship split in two, half of it crashing down in a farm yard. The other part drifted off until men managed to grab a rope which was dangling from it, and fastened it to a stout fencepost. The crew clinging to this section stepped out unhurt. But the fourteen men who had gone down with the half that fell near Ava were dead. Eleven years later an Ava housewife, while weeding in her garden, found the Annapolis class ring of the *Shenandoah's* gallant lieutenant-commander, Zachary Lansdowne. He was born in Greenville, Ohio, and was considered the navy's top authority on lighter-than-air craft. A monument to his memory has been erected near the spot where the disaster occurred.

MORGAN COUNTY, 1818

Named for General Daniel Morgan, who stood beside Washington when he assumed command of the Revolutionary army

THE *Lorena* often steamed up to leave its passengers and cargo at McConnelsville's wharf. It was a busy place and the *Lorena* met many packets, side-wheelers and 100-foot keelboats. They picked up barrels of salt and flour for Kentucky, unloaded iron from Pittsburgh and molasses from New Orleans. The Muskingum River in those days was alive with craft of all kinds, but the favorite was the *Lorena*. Maybe it was because of her name. She was christened for the tear-jerking ballad about a Zanesville maid, Lorena, and her young clergyman lover. The girl's family disapproved of the match and the two were separated forever. But the clergyman never forgot, and later wrote the poem *Lorena*. The verses were put to music and all America, but especially Muskingum River folk, sang them:

> A hundred months have passed, Lorena
> Since last I held thy hand in mine
> And felt thy pulse beat fast, Lorena
> Though mine beat faster far than thine.
> (and so on for many stanzas.)

Morgan County. Lock on the Muskingum River, below Malta and Mc-Connelsville.

Morgan County. View looking up the Muskingum River toward Malta and McConnelsville.

The Muskingum sweeps tranquilly past little villages and sycamore-covered banks. Facing each other on opposite shores are the twin cities of McConnelsville and Malta. McConnelsville, the county seat, was named for the man who founded it in 1817. General McConnel and the men who came with him were from Virginia. They left the stamp of the South in homes and buildings, especially in the yellow and white classic courthouse, which still stands. Settlers built their trim little houses close to sidewalks of criss-crossed brick, giving the village a quaint dignity. McConnelsville, with a population twice Malta's 1,000, was bigger and livelier in the days of river commerce.

The river's drop of more than 100 feet made navigation tricky, and Muskingum River pilots were famous for their skill. Government locks, dams and river canals helped ease the problem. Today, barges loaded with coal and oil still ply the waters, but river traffic is not as great as it once was.

Malta was the home of James Ball Naylor, well known at the turn of the last century for historical novels, most of them with Ohio settings. His sister, Lelia Naylor Morris, though blind for many years, composed 1,500 gospel songs and hymns, including such favorites as *The Stranger of Galilee* and *Nearer, Still Nearer*. . .

MUSKINGUM COUNTY, 1804

Named for the river Muskingum, an Indian word meaning "beside the river"

STOCKY Colonel Ebenezer Zane, wind-brown and strong as an Indian, led his party slowly into the Ohio Country. They followed old paths beaten hard by buffalo and Indian, or chopped their way through the forests. Tomepomehala, their Indian guide, walked ahead, silent most of the time. The colonel's brother Jonathan, experienced woodsman like all the Zanes, was along. John McIntire, Ebenezer's son-in-law, shoemaker by trade, brought up the rear in charge of packhorses bearing food and baggage. It was the summer of 1796, about the time Moses Cleaveland was laying out his city on Lake Erie. But Zane knew nothing of that venture.

He was cutting through the road he had contracted with Congress to lay from Wheeling to Limestone, Kentucky. Years before he had founded Wheeling, and now it was a busy center and jumping-off place for settlers westward bound. They needed a road to carry them into the new lands; the road in turn would benefit his Wheeling holdings. Now he was at work on the highway which he estimated would be about 600 miles in length. When completed, it was little more than a trail, only wide enough for a horse and rider, though travelers and their wagons soon broadened it. It was the first road through the Ohio Country. Men christened it Zane's Trace. For the undertaking Zane was to receive three parcels of land of 640 acres each at the three main river crossings, where he planned to lay out towns.

When he reached the mouth of the Licking where it empties into the Muskingum, Zane reined his horse. This, he decided, would be the site of his first town. Zanesville, today a city of 41,000, is the result. Its present population almost equals that of Lancaster and Chillicothe combined, the other two places where he laid out towns and took his land payment. Zane engaged Rufus Putnam of Marietta as surveyor. Putnam was so impressed with the location that he helped his nephews buy adjoining land, where the future town of Putnam developed, today a part of Zanesville.

After the Trace was cut, Zane went back to Wheeling, deeding the Zanesville lands to his brother Jonathan and McIntire for a hundred dollars. The two ran ferries across the rivers, which was a profitable business since settlers, coming in steady stream, provided them with customers. McIntire, who had learned to cook on the road-making trip, opened a tavern where meals were good and the weary slept on beds instead of on the floor in the usual frontier style.

Zanesville grew, became the county seat and, from 1810 to 1812, was the capital of Ohio. Clay and sand were right for stoneware and glass-making, and a glass factory was established as early as 1815. Pottery and glass are important products today. A Y-bridge was flung across the two rivers in 1814, one of the first such structures in the world. There were four altogether, one after another, including today's steel span. Two were covered. The bridge was the wonder of the frontier, and Zanesville became the Y-Bridge City. Some called it the Wonder City. The rivers, Zane's Trace, the bridge, the canal, the

Muskingum County. Zanesville's Y-bridge spanning the Licking and Muskingum rivers.

National Road and, later, the railroads all came to Zanesville, and the town developed into the hustling, noisy, crowded city of 41,000 it is today. The Muskingum Conservancy Watershed and Dillon Dam on the Licking have harnessed the waters which formerly caused flood problems. A few miles west of Zanesville on the National Road is Headley Inn, built in 1835, which served as a stop for stage and Conestoga wagon passengers, and in the summer months serves modern motorists.

Louisa St. Clair, lovely daughter of the Northwest Territory governor, Arthur St. Clair, galloped after one of her father's scouts who was carrying a letter from the governor to Indians encamped at Duncan Falls. The message invited them to a peace conference at St. Clair's headquarters in Marietta.

"Let me take the letter to the camp," she said. "I know Chief Brant's son. I met him when we were both in Philadelphia at school, and I'm sure I can persuade him to come to the peace meeting."

The scout was indignant: "You can't go to an Indian camp alone!"

In the end, though, Louisa had her way. She was not only received cordially by young Brant, but he accompanied her back to Marietta.

While there he asked the general for her hand in marriage. No one knows how Louisa felt about the proposal, but the general was furious. Brant left in anger. The rest of the legend—one of Ohio's sturdiest— is that two years later Brant was among the tribal leaders who so disastrously defeated St. Clair on the Wabash, but gave orders that the general's life be saved. Perhaps, had a marriage taken place between the distinguished white governor's daughter and the son of an influential Indian leader, Ohio might have been spared decades of bloody Indian warfare.

Zanesville was the home of Zane Grey, descendant of the pioneer Zanes and prolific author of western stories. Grey, a dentist, sold his office equipment to get his first book published. His most famous novel is *Riders of the Purple Sage*, published in 1912. Cass Gilbert, another son of Zanesville, was architect of the Woolworth Building in New York City, for years the tallest building in the world. Jean Starr Untermeyer is Zanesville's best known poet.

LICKING COUNTY, 1808

Named for the numerous local salt licks, much used in early days

IT WAS a shiny new shovel they handed to Governor De Witt Clinton on July 4, 1825. That spade changed the history of Ohio and of the United States. Hundreds of men, women and children in wagons and on horseback had come to Licking Summit near Newark to see the long-awaited canal officially started. Eager as they were for it, they could not then imagine how great its contribution would be in bringing settlers and commerce to Ohio and the West. Clinton, governor of New York State, lauded for its Erie Canal, had clattered into Newark that morning on a stage from Cleveland. He stuck his spade in the ground, lifted a bit of earth and dumped it in a wheelbarrow. A terrific shout went up. The canal was begun! He handed the implement to Jeremiah Morrow, Ohio governor, who dug up more dirt amid louder cheering.

The pioneer farmers hung around after the ceremony was over.

Unable to market their produce they were desperate for income. Maybe they could get work on-the new canal. The wages sounded good to men who had almost forgotten the feel of real money. Pay, they heard, started at $8 for twenty-six working days a month, with lodging and whisky thrown in. As labor became more scarce, the standard pay went up slightly. That same day in St. Clairsville, 100 miles to the east, the National Road was started with similar ceremonies. Both the road and the canal shaped Ohio.

Newark's population, 500 at the time of Clinton's visit, grew in the next ten years to nearly 3,000. Its 1950 census was 35,000. Glass-making, occupation of pioneer days, has remained a leading industry, and an important plant today turns out carload lots of products fashioned from the new glass fibre substance. Newark, county seat, was named for Newark, New Jersey, home of the first settlers. They found many Mound Builder embankments such as Eagle Mound and the 100-acre Octagon Mound, probably designed for ceremonials connected with the sun. Both are within state parks. To the south lies Flint Ridge, which supplied high-grade stone for Indian arrowheads and was open territory respected by all tribes. Remains found here indicate it was visited by Indians from far-distant places.

At Jacksontown, not far away, is Dawes Arboretum, established by Mr. and Mrs. B. G. Dawes in 1929. On 500 acres 1,300 varieties of trees are grown, many of them descendants of historic trees like the Charter Oak where Connecticut's charter was hidden from the royal governor in the seventeenth century, and Ohio's Logan Elm, ancient tree near Circleville under which Chief Logan in the 1770s made his eloquent indictment of the white man's cruelties to his race.

Long before the traveler reaches Granville he sees the lofty tower of Denison University's Memorial Chapel, one of the numerous handsome campus buildings on the encircling ridge. Denison, begun in 1831 as the Granville Literary and Theological Institution, received its present name more than twenty years later when a well-to-do farmer, William Denison, agreed to donate $10,000 if the college was named after him. This was agreed upon, but differences arose. Denison paid only part of his pledge, refusing the balance despite suits brought by the college to collect.

Few Ohio towns are as appealing as Granville. Its principal street,

Licking County. Dominating the landscape for miles is the tower of the Swasey Memorial Chapel of Denison University at Granville. In the foreground is the college observatory.

Broadway, 100 feet from curb to curb, is lined with fine old trees, classic homes and public buildings. In 1804 nearly all the citizens of Granville, Massachusetts, moved here, first forming themselves into a Congregational Church. Their first act on reaching Ohio was to fell a tree, chip the stump into a pulpit and hold divine services in the woods. When they started the first hymn, some could not continue for weeping. The song was heard over the hill by Theophilus Reese, a Welshman, searching at the moment for a lost cow. Though he understood no English, he sensed the religious note, and thanked his God that at last he was to have Christian neighbors.

A narrow strip called the Refugee Tract extended over southern Licking, adjoining Franklin, Fairfield and Perry Counties, as far west as Columbus and including Buckeye Lake. This was a 58,000-acre tract set aside by Congress to reimburse those British in Canada and Nova Scotia who had sympathized with the American cause during the Revolutionary War and lost their properties as a result.

FAIRFIELD COUNTY, 1800

Named for the lovely rolling land

"TAKE Cump, the red-headed one —he's the brightest."

Mary Sherman in her modest, heavily mortgaged home resolutely faced her new widowhood. Her caller was big Tom Ewing, her husband's devoted friend and frequent companion on the lawyer's circuit, the Stirrup Court. He and his wife lived nearby on Lancaster's East Main Street hill. They wanted to help by taking one of the eleven Sherman children. The families were intimate and their children were like brothers and sisters. Cump was nine that day in 1829.

Cump's real name was Tecumseh, for the great Indian chief whom the Shermans knew and admired. The child was called in from play. He listened solemnly, pushing his always unruly hair from his eyes. Soon he was packing his few possessions. He tucked the neat bundle under one arm, trustingly clasped Ewing's huge hand and walked from the crowded house where he was born up the hill to his big new home. William was given to Cump as a first name when Mrs. Ewing, a devout Catholic, had him baptized, with the consent of his Presbyterian mother. The priest would not countenance the "heathen" Tecumseh. Years later Sherman married Ewing's daughter, Ellen, in the big house. Guests at the wedding were the President of the United States and his cabinet, senators, Supreme Court justices, Daniel Webster, Henry Clay. Sherman's birthplace is now a state museum, a memorial to General William Tecumseh Sherman whose generalship helped end the Civil War and save the Union. His most famous campaign, the march through Georgia, he planned in the Ewing homestead while home on a furlough.

Lancaster, county seat of Fairfield County, was put on the map—literally—by that great American road builder, Ebenezer Zane, whose Trace, chopped out of the wilderness from Wheeling to Kentucky, passed through the site of present-day Lancaster. Zane established the village, calling it first New Lancaster in deference to some squatters already there from Lancaster, Pennsylvania. Here Wyandot Indians had a big village, Tahre Town, with 100 wigwams clustered under Standing Stone. Today, as Mt. Pleasant, it is a favorite picnic spot. On its summit the glamorous Rose Forester was captured by the Indians. She was rescued romantically by a sharpshooting scout who married her.

A cemetery on the edge of Lancaster belongs to the Presidents of the United States. A ten-sided high stone wall encloses ground which Nathaniel Wilson in 1817 "bequeathed to James Monroe, president of the United States and his successors in office forever" hoping they would be buried beside the grave Wilson ultimately occupied.

St. John's Episcopal Church, built in 1848, linked Ohio's Lancaster with the Duke of Lancaster and the War of the Roses fought four hundred years before in England. Plaster roses painted white, color of the Duke of York, are sprinkled over the church auditorium ceiling which is red, color of the House of Lancaster in that war. Near St. John's are many of the city's magnificent old houses, beautifully maintained. The canal, promoted by Ewing, brought the wealth that built the homes. A second boom came with the discovery of natural gas in the 1880s. This city of 25,000 lists glass-making as its biggest single industry.

Fairfield County. Library built by Mabel Wagnalls Jones in Lithopolis.

Fairfield County. Old covered bridges are numerous in the county.

A college education for four years, and as much post-graduate study as one wishes, is available to those who live in Bloom Township and have graduated from any of the three high schools serving the area. This liberal scholarship opportunity is administered in Lithopolis, village of 300, by trustees of the will of Mabel Wagnalls Jones. She was the daughter of Adam Wagnalls of the publishing firm Funk & Wagnalls, New York City. In 1925 she built a half-million-dollar Tudor-Gothic library in the village. At her death in 1946 the library received a $2,500,000 endowment. The library and scholarships are in memory of Mrs. Jones' parents, natives of the village. Its Greek name means "city of stone," an appropriate name since a strata of rock underlies the spot. No other village of this size in the world dispenses so much money for education and books.

DELAWARE COUNTY, 1808

Named for Algonquin Indians living along the Delaware River. They moved into Ohio in the 1700s.

SOPHIA HAYES' brother, Sardis Birchard, was only sixteen in 1822, the year her baby Rutherford was born and her husband died. Sardis became the family head, cheerfully shouldering responsibility for the widow and her baby as well as the two older children. Sardis had been cared for by his sister and her husband when his parents died, and now he could show his gratitude. The young uncle worked at whatever jobs he could find. However, Delaware developed too slowly for Sardis who, a handsome bachelor at twenty-one, was ambitious and impatient. Deciding he could make a better living for his sister and her brood, he moved them all to Lower Sandusky, later renamed Fremont. He soon became a leader in the new community. His nephew Rutherford, whom he called "Rud," was his favorite among his sister's children. His uncle gave him every advantage, and he went from one success to another. The site of the little house on Williams Street in Delaware where they all lived is now marked with a plaque as the birthplace of Rutherford Birchard Hayes who, in 1877, became the nineteenth president of the United States.

Delaware County. Stone barn near Stratford, embellished with hex signs. Now mere decoration, these magic symbols were originally employed to ward off evil and the spells of witches.

The city, like the county, took its name from the Delaware Indians who worked large acres of corn here. Remnants of the tribe remained in the vicinity for years. Their presence led to continual but groundless rumors of Indian attack and kept the settlement in turmoil. One of them, Chief Leatherlips, lived in the Olentangy Caverns, a string of limestone caves thought to be formed by a prehistoric underground river. Wyandots, objecting to his friendship with whites, condemned him to death. Accepting the sentence calmly, he ate a good meal of jerked deer meat and dressed himself in his best beaded buckskin. At the cave entrance he knelt before his captors and one of them stepped forward and sank a tomahawk in his skull.

The many mineral springs attracted the Indians and later the pioneers. "Water curing" was popular, and in the 1830s an elaborate spa was developed in the town of Delaware. It failed in a few years and Ohio Methodists bought the property at the bargain price of

$10,000. They remodeled the large hotel, the Mansion House, and founded Ohio Wesleyan University in 1842, turning the resort grounds into a campus. Despite intervals of financial stress the college went ahead as the bastion of Ohio Methodism. In 1877 it became co-educational by union with Ohio Wesleyan Female College and its scope and prestige broadened. Delaware, the county seat, has a population of 11,000 and revolves around the university. One of the county landmarks is the Perkins Observatory, pushing impressively above the treetops south of Delaware. It is named for Hiram Perkins, a gifted astronomer, and is used both by Ohio Wesleyan and Ohio State University at Columbus.

The county has many mellow old buildings built of quarried blue limestone or the soft-colored river stone. Along the Olentangy are ruins of stone ghost mills and houses, overrun by twining vines and dark green moss. Stratford is a lovely "stone village." Its original name is said to have been Stratford-on-Olentangy, after Stratford-on-Avon, England. There is a picturesque stone church and in the country are numerous stone barns. Many of these are embellished with "hex signs," curious Old-World symbols, some shaped like swastikas and half moons, guaranteed to ward off evil spirits. Around Radnor an early Welsh settlement developed, and much Welsh tradition survives in the pleasant rural districts.

FRANKLIN COUNTY, 1803

Named for Benjamin Franklin

OHIO'S capital was to move again! News of the Assembly act flashed through the wilderness. It was to be within 40 miles of the center of the state, and this time a permanent site. Ohio never was quite satisfied with Chillicothe, the seat of government since 1803. Selection of Zanesville, 1810–1812, was temporary, everyone knew, though the town had built a magnificent statehouse, something like Philadelphia's Independence Hall. Now the legislature was once more back in Chillicothe, choosing the final capital so all this moving about could stop.

Every town within the designated radius, hoping to be the chosen one, sent prominent citizens to scheme and bargain with the lawmakers. Farmers looked over their fields and saw, wishfully, in place of the stumps and fenceposts, a majestic capital city. They galloped off to lay their vision before the legislature. It looked as if Dublin was winning out, when the announcement came in 1812. The new capital would be on the high bank of the Scioto opposite Franklinton. A four-man syndicate agreed to erect a statehouse and other necessary public buildings on two 10-acre lots for $50,000. In 1816 the new statehouse opened. It was square with a towered cupola like those at Chillicothe and Zanesville. Open fireplaces set with brass andirons furnished heat from wood cut on the grounds. Adjacent building lots sold rapidly even though they were covered with forests and swamps. The new town was named Columbus.

State business increased. Soon a bigger capitol was needed. In 1839 the design of the present building was accepted following the commissioners' tour of eastern cities and a contest in which 50 architects participated. Planned to be six years in construction at a price of $400,000, instead it was completed twenty-two years later at a cost of $1,644,000. But it was "the largest and finest of any state capitol." It is called one of the best examples of Greek Doric in the country.

Columbus reached 376,000 in 1950. It is the county seat and a city of varied living patterns, with the political in the lead. At the north end is Ohio State University's 2,100-acre campus. With an enrollment of 18,500, it is the largest college in Ohio. It opened in 1873 as the Ohio Agricultural and Mechanical College. On its campus is the museum and headquarters of the Ohio State Archaeological and Historical Society. Capital University, under Lutheran auspices, is another educational institution. Columbus is likewise a cultural center with many outstanding libraries including the Ohio State Library, the fine libraries of the University and historical society, and the Martha Kinney Cooper Ohioana Library devoted to works by Ohioans. Fort Hayes is a trim little municipality within Columbus city limits. Columbus handles diverse and vigorous civilian industries. Manufacturing got under way in the horse and buggy days when 23 factories made carriages and wagons which were shipped to world markets.

Franklin County. Home of the World League Against Alcohol in Westerville, formerly the Anti-Saloon League.

Worthington and Westerville, two mellow old towns to the north, retain their individuality though practically suburbs of Columbus. At Worthington is the only college in America directly under Pope Pius XII, the Pontifical College Josephinum, a seminary for priests. There are only two others like it, one in Africa, the other in Mexico. The college is an outgrowth of an orphanage established in Pomeroy in 1870 by Father Joseph Jessing. His ventures were supported by contributions from German-speaking Catholics. A training school for priests evolved and Father Jessing offered his new seminary to Rome. The college was moved to Worthington in the 1930s. Among its alumni are 400 priests in 80 dioceses throughout the country.

Westerville became the "Dry Capital" of America in 1909 when citizens donated a big house as headquarters for the Anti-Saloon League. During the "Dry Decades" politicians courted league leaders, especially its Ohio-born legal head and astute lobbyist, Wayne B.

Franklin County. The State House at Columbus.

Wheeler. With repeal of prohibition the old brick house remained the home of dry forces, under the new name of the League Against Alcohol. In a plant on the grounds temperance literature is published in many languages and distributed throughout the world.

Otterbein College, also situated in Westerville, was founded on a 40-acre campus by the United Brethren Church in 1847 and was one of the first colleges in Ohio to admit women as students. Hanby House adjoining the campus was the Westerville home of Benjamin Hanby, author of *Darling Nellie Gray* and other old-time song hits. It is furnished throughout with Hanby mementoes and is open to the public.

Another song writer, Oley Speaks, was born in Canal Winchester. He is known particularly for his *On the Road to Mandalay, Sylvia* and *When the Boys Come Marching Home.* He was also a concert baritone and lived for many years in Columbus.

HOCKING COUNTY, 1818

Named for Hockhocking River, Indian word meaning "bottleneck"

FLAMES OF the big council fire leaped 100 feet against the ceiling of the cave. The reflection danced over the faces of a couple of hundred Indians sitting cross-legged in solemn war powwow. Ohioans named the huge rock mouth Ash Cave because of the ashes of those campfires which have made the floor— thousands of bushels of dry, hard ashes. It is one of the entrancing sights of Ohio's "Little Yellowstone," otherwise Hocking State Forest in southern Hocking County. In the 5,000 acres of scenic woodlands the state maintains public recreation areas and is carrying on a vast reforestation program. Not far away is Old Man's Cave, a great hollowed-out opening with an overhanging rock roof 100 feet above its platform. Beside it a creek splashes in a ravine, and high above this hurrying water, nature carved the profile of a man. The cave gets its name from this, or from the long-haired ragged old hermit who, local lore says, used to live in its depths. Cedar Falls drops hundreds of feet into a crystal pool that appears bottomless, its wet roar breaking the forest stillness. Most dramatic of all is Rock House, a cathedral-like arrangement of gigantic sandstone blocks. Sunlight filters through fissures to cavernous rooms with Gothic-like window openings, and doorways arched by the ages. Lichens and ferns hang from the rock walls, sprayed by countless little waterfalls. Water thrushes splash about in the streams, and swallows and phoebes nest in the rock cavities. At dusk and at dawn the whippoorwill endlessly repeats his call. Mingoes and Shawnees once roamed the country and hid captives in the caves. Horse thieves stabled their animals in the hollows, and many a desperado dodged the law in these wild depths.

Hocking Park's primeval beauty is unspoiled. The area is part of the 145,000 acres officially designated as state park land. Good automobile highways and miles of hiking paths make every part accessible and more than 50,000 persons visit it annually.

County seat Logan, a city of 6,000, calls itself with just pride "the Gateway to Ohio's Wonderland." Until the canal came in 1840 it was

Hocking County. One of many natural beauty spots in Hocking State Park.

isolated. Later a railroad opened it further to trade. For many years it was the center of a brisk coal mining business which declined following the disastrous New Straitsville underground mine fire. The city was named by its founder, Colonel Thomas Worthington, for the great Mingo, Chief Logan.

PERRY COUNTY, 1817

Named for Admiral Oliver Hazard Perry

"LITTLE PHIL," astride a prancing horse, waves his cavalry hat to all who pass through Somerset. Though speeding motorists grumble and truckers complain, they must drive around the statue of General Philip Sheridan in the center of the square. Somerset is proud of this small general of the Civil War and likes to look up at him, forever charging ahead, for they recall the words of the poem by Thomas Buchanan Read, "Sheridan's Ride":

> Up from the South at break of day
> Bringing to Winchester fresh dismay.

That was in 1864 when Sheridan rode 20 miles at breakneck speed from a conference with Grant at Winchester to rescue his forces from defeat. It was one of the exploits that ranked him a cavalry genius. Sheridan was born in 1831 in New York on the Erie Canal where his Irish father was a laborer. The family came to Somerset when Phil was a baby. The village renamed the street where he grew up Sheridan, in his honor. Somerset citizens point out the stores on the square where he clerked as a boy to augment his father's slim income. After the Civil War Sheridan was Reconstruction ruler of Texas and Louisiana where he was hated for his stern policies. He built a charming Gothic Revival style home in Somerset for his parents. It is now a private residence.

The spires of one of Ohio's oldest Catholic churches, St. Joseph's, are seen in the quiet country outside Somerset. Bishop Edward Fenwick, when a humble Dominican missionary, built the first log church. Today's stately edifice has windows of exquisite Munich glass and

Perry County. The subterranean fire which has burned in a coal mine at New Straitsville since 1884.

valuable relics like the gold and scarlet vestments originally given to a fifteenth-century Spanish church by Ferdinand V. Somerset, though no longer the county seat, cherishes its old Virginia-style courthouse on the square. Over its classic door is the motto with the garbled wording: "Let Justice be done if the Heavens fall." Stone masons indifferent to the changed meaning chiseled in "if" because they lacked space for the proper "though."

New Lexington, the present county seat, has a population of 4,300, three times as large as Somerset. In the New Lexington cemetery is a monument to its most famous son, Januarius Aloysius MacGahan, war correspondent of the 1870s. He adopted Russia as his home, living at the Czar's court, riding like a Cossack with Russian armies. His dispatches about Turkish barbarities in Bulgaria stirred the world. When the country was freed by Russia he rode with the liberating armies. Bulgaria celebrated his birthday as a national holiday. In 1870, during the Franco-Prussian War which he reported, his boyhood neighbor Sheridan was American military observer.

In New Straitsville, once a busy mining town, potatoes are dug pre-baked; water runs hot in the creeks and vegetation is scorched. The reason is a subterranean fire, creeping through an estimated 30 miles of coal mines, which has burned since 1884. Feathery wisps of smoke and steam, as well as gusts of flames, burst through the earth. The fire was started during a bitter strike when disgruntled miners lighted oil-saturated cars of coal and sent them down the shaft. Countless attempts to extinguish the blaze have been made in vain. Coal valued at many millions has been destroyed, and the district has lost its main source of livelihood. Thus has disregard of public property by a few brought utter waste and hardship to a whole area.

VI North Central

INTRODUCTION

THE EIGHT counties within this group extend in practically a straight line from Lake Erie to the central part of the state. Ottawa, Seneca and Wyandot counties take their names from the Indians who once roamed within their boundaries. In the history of these counties we encounter epics of Indian warfare, and meet some of the most colorful personalities of the Ohio frontier. Within the area occurred young Oliver Perry's defeat of the entire British fleet, and the exploit of another youth, Croghan, who defended a fort with a single cannon—heroic dramas these, to be remembered as long as there is an America.

OTTAWA COUNTY, 1840

Name from an Indian word, tawa, meaning "trader"

IN THE heavy stillness of a hazy September day in 1813, two flotillas of battered ships lay at anchor off a wild and beautiful island. Decks were littered with wreckage and sails hung tattered by shot. The dirge for the dead sounded. British and American sailors carried ashore the bodies of six officers—three American, three British—and buried them on the lonely island shore. Some of the men wore bloody bandages and limped. The day before they had leveled their squadrons' guns at each other in the terrible Battle of Lake Erie, the handsome American commodore, Oliver Hazard Perry, aged twenty-eight, had defeated the entire British fleet.

Before the engagement Perry's nine ships had put in near South Bass Island, thereafter called Put in Bay. Sighting the British, he hoisted over his flagship, the *Lawrence,* a large banner of blue bunting which he himself had made. His crew cheered when they read the words: "Don't Give Up the Ship." It was the last message of his friend James Lawrence, killed the previous June in a naval engagement with the British in Boston harbor. When the enemy pounded the *Lawrence* almost to sinking, Perry grabbed his banner and with his thirteen-year-old brother, his aide, he ordered four seamen to row him to the Niagara. They made it through the gunfire. Perry unfurled the banner over his new ship, and went on with the fight. When it was all over, three long hours after its start, Perry wrote General William Henry Harrison: "Dear General: We have met the enemy and they are ours, two ships, two brigs, one schooner and one sloop. Yours, O. H. Perry." Congress gave him a $5,000 honor award, and $7,100 as his share of the estimated value of the captured British ships. In 1819, while on a diplomatic cruise, he died of yellow fever in Trinidad. His "Don't Give Up the Ship" flag is enshrined at Annapolis.

The British and American officers who died in Perry's battle still sleep in Put in Bay. They are now entombed within the 350-foot granite Peace Monument. It was dedicated on the 100th anniversary of the conflict to honor Perry and to mark a century of peace with Great Britain. The greensward around it is a national park. Tens of thousands of visitors climb to its top each year to look out toward Canada over Lake Erie's waters.

On tiny Gibraltar Island, dropped within the South Bass harbor, Ohio State University maintains the Franz Theodore Stone Institute of Hydrobiology, one of the few freshwater laboratories in existence.

Middle Bass devotes its time to grape-growing and a large winery which looks like an Old-World German rathskeller. At one time the island was the holiday retreat of United States presidents Rutherford B. Hayes, Grover Cleveland, Benjamin Harrison and William Howard Taft.

On the wide-flung arm of Marblehead Peninsula and Catawba Island, the latter not an island at all but also a peninsula, is Lakeside. Outgrowth of a Methodist camp meeting of the 1870s it is Ohio's Chautauqua and annually attracts 65,000 visitors. On the peninsula tip, washed by ocean-high waves, stands Marblehead Lighthouse, built in 1821 and the oldest lighthouse in Ohio.

Port Clinton, county seat, lies in the hollow hand of the harbor. It is busiest in summer when fishing and fruits are at their peak, and when holiday tourists flock through the region. In 1825, shipwrecked immigrants bound for Illinois decided to go no further. They founded Port Clinton whose 5,600 population makes it the largest town in the county. It was named for Governor De Witt Clinton of New York State. Often heard in this section are the guns from Camp Perry, extensive post of the Ohio National Guard where Ohio militia units train each year.

Ottawa County. The annual summer regatta at Put in Bay, Lake Erie. The Perry Memorial Shaft can be seen to the right; Gibraltar Island is in the foreground to the left.

SANDUSKY COUNTY, 1820

Named for the river Sandusky; an old Indian word

Up from the river in steady stream marched the British redcoat regulars and the Indians under Tecumseh. Twelve hundred strong! Would there never be an end to them? The major looking down on this scene from Fort Stephenson that August day in 1813 was George Croghan, a name that is magic still in Sandusky County. He was twenty-one, had less than 200 men, one cannon affectionately dubbed Betsy, and an order from his superior, General William Henry Harrison, to surrender the fort. But a few hours before, Croghan had sent out a scout with an answer to the general: "Message received too late. We mean to hold out." It was reckless disobedience, he knew. Now, somehow, he had to make good.

"Boys, we've got to make 'em think Betsy's a hundred cannons. We'll fire her from every opening." Frantically the men loaded, fired and wheeled her; again and again Betsy was so hot they scarcely could touch her. Enemy artillery answered, came closer, closer! Then Croghan hazarded the shrewd guess which made him famous. Watching the maneuvering, he decided the attack would be aimed at one particular corner of the fort, and there he ordered his men to push Betsy into position. "Fill her with all the powder she'll hold and anything else you can lay your hands on!" After the ammunition they tossed in scrap iron, broken gun parts, nails. Breathlessly Croghan kept his eyes on the swarms outside. He was right. British and Indians were massing as he expected! "Fire away!" he yelled. Betsy spewed her contents on ranks not thirty yards away. Croghan lost one man. Outside the fort were 150 dead British, and more dying, with the rest scurrying to their boats on the Sandusky River. When a runner carried the news to Harrison, he tore up the court-martial papers he had prepared against Croghan and wrote a message to Congress commending him.

The Croghan story is the great saga of Fremont, the county seat. The site of the fort is the heart of the modern city. The body of the major, re-interred here in 1906, lies beneath a tall monument which looks out toward the river whence his enemies came, and went. Guarding him forever is his cannon, "Old Betsy."

On the fort site is another beloved Fremont landmark, Birchard Public Library. It was founded in 1870, when public libraries were rare in Ohio, by Sardis Birchard. He settled here in 1827 when this was Lower Sandusky, and made money in pioneer ventures. His prosperity was the town's for he was the moving spirit in all civic ventures. A bachelor, he and his nephew Rutherford Birchard Hayes were as close as father and son, closer than many.

Birchard and his nephew led the agitation to change the town's name. Lower Sandusky was too often confused with Upper Sandusky and Sandusky City. It was the time of the Forty-niners and John C. Fremont's western explorations. Fremont, the choice of Hayes, won out. Croghan would have been selected but for the variations in pronunciations, one as if the word were spelled "Crawn"!

In 1850 Birchard developed a home for himself and his nephew in a 25-acre woodland on the edge of the city. The little rainwater pools reminded him of mirrors. He called the place Spiegel (German for mirror) Grove.

Hayes, his wife Lucy and their children came whenever Hayes could get away from his busy Cincinnati law practice, his duties as congressman and later his obligations as governor. In 1873 the Hayes family moved to the Grove permanently. It was none too soon. Uncle Sardis had only one more year of life left. He missed what would have been his greatest thrill, the inauguration in 1877 of his nephew as President of the United States. After his term in the White House, Hayes and his family returned to Spiegel Grove to live.

Hayes' large library, greatly expanded, and his papers and documents are housed at Spiegel Grove in the Hayes Memorial Library. Built by Hayes' son, Webb C. Hayes, and the state of Ohio, it is open to the public and much used by students of the Hayes era. The spacious home was retained by Hayes' descendants as a private residence, and is now the home of the president's grandson, Webb C. Hayes II, and his wife.

When Sandusky County needed a bigger courthouse it enlarged its fine old Greek Revival structure without changing the original architecture.

138

Sandusky County. Monument to Major George Croghan, hero of the War of 1812, on the grounds of the Birchard Public Library, Fremont.

Clyde, city of 4,000, erected a handsome monument over the grave of General James B. McPherson, killed at thirty-five near Atlanta in 1834. The engaging McPherson was the son of a local blacksmith, and very popular. Many tourists visit the grave. Clyde was the boyhood home of Sherwood Anderson, American writer born in Camden, in Preble County.

Many thousands of acres of this and surrounding counties, particularly those to the west, are given over to sugar beets, cucumbers and cabbages as well as cherry orchards. Every spring armies of migrant workers, mostly Texans of Spanish descent, arrive to cultivate and harvest the crops, and return to their homes in the fall. In the towns and cities throughout this section are a number of sugar factories as well as canneries processing the fruit, making sauerkraut and pickles.

SENECA COUNTY, 1824

Named for Seneca Indians who had a reservation within its limits

WHEN Charlie Foster started clerking in his father's store he was so little he had to stand on a cheese box to reach the counter. The store occupied one half of a log building and the other side was the Fosters' home. It was in the midst of the Black Swamp, an area of impassable roads and a breeding ground for the ague. The store was near Rome and Risdon, two settlements so jealous of each other's growth that citizens of one seldom passed those from the other without stopping for a good fist fight. Differences, however, were forgotten by 1854, and the two united as one town called Fostoria in honor of the storekeeper C. W. Foster, whose place by now was the biggest country store in Ohio.

In 1880 the Republicans nominated Foster's son for the Ohio governorship. Democrats jeered at him as "Calico Charlie," but this ridicule of his storekeeping days did not prevent his being elected, and re-elected for a second term. The town named for his father spread beyond Seneca County into Wood and Sandusky Counties as well.

An early plank road, laid with the greatest difficulty through the mucklands, and later in 1859 a pioneer railroad, launched Fostoria toward its modern prosperity as a shipping center. The heart of the city today is crossed by ground-level tracks of half a dozen railroad lines. In addition to factories and busy stockyards, Fostoria is the home of an unusual business, a nationally known firm which writes and stages benefit plays and historical community pageants for amateur actors.

Josiah Hedges laid out a town along the Sandusky River in 1820 and called it Tiffin for his friend and fellow-Virginian, Edward Tiffin of Chillicothe, the first governor of Ohio. The name brought luck to the town, but not immediately. Before Hedges' arrival, a soldier of the War of 1812 had stopped at Fort Ball, on the opposite bank from the future Tiffin, and vowed: "If I live through this bloody war, I'll come back and build me a tavern here." A few years later he did just

Seneca County. Heidelberg College, founded in 1850, occupies a large campus in the heart of Tiffin. Founders' Hall was the first building.

that. The settlement that developed around him he called Oakley. It became a bitter rival of the new Tiffin. The Sandusky River that lay between them did its best to keep the feud alive by spilling over in periodic floods, and destroying every bridge connecting the two. However, Tiffin became the county seat, and soon swallowed up Oakley.

Today Tiffin, an industrial city of 19,000, lies on both banks, landscaped with anti-flood retaining walls, and spanned by graceful bridges. The town's layout, architecture and traditions bear the stamp of its two early pioneer strains, Southern and German. Houses in simple classic lines, built by descendants of Virginia founders, were often of brick as an early brick-making machine had been invented here. Germans made money in breweries and built many of the large houses that distinguish the city. Tiffin was hit by the gas boom of the late 1880s which struck neighboring districts.

The Germans in 1850 founded Heidelberg College, named for the famed university of their homeland. It is under the auspices of the Evangelical and Reformed church and now occupies a 35-acre campus in the heart of the city.

In front of the county courthouse is the statue of General William H. Gibson. The stone figure means little to today's throngs who pass him daily, but during his lifetime no one thought of Tiffin without also calling Gibson to mind. In the days before amplifiers he was in demand as a speaker at political rallies and patriotic gatherings because his voice could be heard by acres of listeners gathered in parks and open fields. He had not only lung power but eloquence as well, and his hearers felt cheated if his speeches were less than two and a half hours long.

At Tiffin for years was the 1,000-acre orphanage of the Junior Order of the United American Mechanics. The grounds and buildings now are state-owned, the Tiffin State Hospital for the mentally ill. Old-time county traditions and relics are preserved in the Seneca County Museum on Clay Street, in a fine old house built by a Virginia-born early merchant.

HANCOCK COUNTY, 1828

Named for John Hancock, first signer of the Declaration of Independence

FOR THREE days and nights 30,000 gas jets burned on 58 flower- and flag-festooned arches over Findlay's

Main Street. It was the Gas Jubilee of 1887, one of the most fantastic celebrations ever staged in Ohio. Bands played, rockets went off. Parades and floats streamed through the streets while marchers were pelted with flowers. Pouring into the city by wagon, carriage and train, over 40,000 visitors came to witness the spectacle.

The orgy marked the peak of frenzied speculation over gas which lay like an airy ocean under Findlay and adjoining townships. For forty years before the boom, there had been tales of gas which puffed shovels out of the hands of men digging basements, and knocked fenceposts out of holes. Citizens did not take the gas seriously until one day the great Karg well "came in." Its roar was like that of a fast express, and its flame shot 200 feet in the air. It was winter, but with warm weather ground around the well was thawed and became covered with green grass.

Derricks grew on the landscape like trees, and fortunes were made in a day. Manufacturers, seeing cheap fuel ahead, rushed in from faraway cities, the gas ran out, and it was 1910 before Findlay, calmed and recovered, was laying the foundations for today's half a hundred vigorous industries including manufacturing of petroleum products, a business which developed when oil took the place of gas in local wells. The city's 1950 census of 24,000 is larger than in gas boom days. Findlay was named for Colonel James Findlay, who commanded a regiment under General Hull and marched through here on his way to Detroit in the War of 1812.

Through Hancock County's long stretches of farm country, the Blanchard River meanders. Nobody would call it one of Ohio's important streams, but millions have sung about it. On its banks stood the old Misamore Mill. Tell Taylor, born on a farm near it, used to swim and fish in the mill race. He had a good voice, sang in the Presbyterian Church choir, sometimes put on amateur musicals, and wrote songs. One song about childhood haunts around the mill he called *Down by the Old Mill Stream*. He did not think much of it, but he gave it to some friends who begged for a song for their vaudeville act. It made an astonishing hit, and when he published it more than 5,000,000 copies were sold. Taylor organized his own music company in Chicago. There he collaborated with the Cleveland composer, Ernest Ball, famous for his *Mother Machree, Love Me and the*

Hancock County. The Blanchard River near Findlay inspired the composer Tell Taylor to write *Down by the Old Mill Stream.*

World Is Mine, and many other songs. Later, Taylor went into musical comedy with Weber and Fields, writing many of their acts. Among his other successes were *Rock Me to Sleep in the Old Rocking Chair, If Dreams Come True* and *He Sleeps Beneath the Soil of France.*

A Cincinnati coachman, attracted to Findlay by the promises of gas, was left penniless when the boom passed. He turned to an odd business, mask-making, the trade of his family in Germany. Today one of Findlay's small but busy factories turns out many thousands of masks, which are used in many parts of the country for schoolroom dramatics, Mardi Gras events and street parades.

At the outbreak of the Civil War an itinerant printer got a job on the Findlay *Jeffersonian.* One day, a little item appeared about "Petroleum Vesuvius Nasby, late pastor uv the Church uv the New Dispensation." Thereafter there were daily articles in bad spelling and grammar, apparently sympathetic to the South's cause, but with wry humor actually making fun of the Confederates. The author was David Ross Locke. He moved on to the Toledo *Blade,* later becoming its owner, but he continued his "dispatches" as long as he lived. He was one of America's most popular humorists. One of his avid readers was Lincoln, who is said to have read a Nasby letter to his cabinet before preparing his Emancipation Proclamation.

HARDIN COUNTY, 1833

Named for Colonel John Hardin, veteran of the Revolution, killed near today's Hardin, Shelby County

THE county commissioners dismounted at old Fort McArthur and stamped the stiffness from their legs. As they pushed open the blockhouse door at the fort they sniffed hungrily at the promising odor of wild turkey turning before the hearth fire. The county, laid out so long ago, finally was being organized formally. The men were about to pick a county seat.

"We're agreed, I take it, to lay out the town near here. But what are we going to call it?" Some suggested Hardin, for young Colonel John Hardin, brutally massacred by Ohio Indians while on a peace mission to them. But his name had been given to the county, and the others did not want to use it for the town too.

One of the women, preparing a meal for the commissioners, interrupted. "I've heard your talk about a name for the new town. What'd ye think of Kenton? For Simon Kenton. He's tramped through here a hundred times. My father used to hunt with him and I've heard him say there never was a sharper Indian scout nor a kinder man. He's still alive, past eighty, living over in Zanesfield. He'd be mighty set up to have a town named for him. . . ."

The commissioners knew Kenton as everyone in that section did, and they liked the idea. So in 1833 Kenton was given a place on the Ohio map. The old fort has since disappeared, but the city, grown to 9,000 in 1950, is the biggest town in the county. Today, though there are a few small industries, Kenton is mostly a trade center for the surrounding fine farming districts.

Hardin County. Simon Kenton, colorful frontier scout and Indian fighter, whose name was given to Kenton, the county seat.

Simon Kenton passed through here when he was fifty; he was a sergeant under General Hull during the War of 1812. The soldiers' route along North Washington Street is marked by huge slices of stone pillars from the former classic county courthouse which was replaced by a larger structure now on Courthouse Square.

Kenton's frequent companion, Daniel Boone, is the better known of the two in American annals. Yet Kenton's exploits were more harrowing, and it is odd that he has not become the traditional hero of the American boy. The factual chronicle of his life is more exciting than fiction. Kenton was born in 1755 in Virginia in the same place and almost the same year as John Hardin. He fled from home as a youth, thinking, mistakenly, that he had killed a man with whom he had fought over a girl both loved. Assuming the name Simon Butler as a disguise, Kenton wandered from Kentucky into Ohio and back again, embroiled in the Indian warfare which was the western campaign of the Revolutionary War. Fleet of foot and of wit, powerful in body, and at home in the woods, he was in demand as a scout. Though usually he outsmarted the Indians, now and then he was captured. During one long captivity he was condemned on several occasions to be burned at the stake, but each time was saved by pleas of friends. Kenton lore abounds in western Ohio. Once Indians strapped him to the back of a fast horse. The animal raced with him through the forest until the clothes were torn from his body, and he was left bruised almost to death. More than once he "ran the gantlet." Somehow Kenton lived through it all and, despite his sufferings, retained an affection for the Indians who returned it. In his old age a retinue of Indians was always with him, and he shared with them his twenty-dollar-a-month government pension. After his death in 1836 he was buried in Urbana, scene of many of his adventures.

Ada is the seat of learning for Hardin County. Ohio Northern University is the materialization of the dream of a young schoolteacher, Henry Solomon Lehr. When he was discharged from the Union Army at the close of the Civil War, he was so disturbed over the low caliber of teacher training that he persuaded the town fathers of Ada to let him start a private normal school in an abandoned schoolhouse. Lush and lean years followed. The college righted itself, however, and today it has a curriculum that is varied but still specializes in Lehr's ideas of "training teachers in the science of education."

WYANDOT COUNTY, 1845

Named for Wyandot Indians

COLONEL WILLIAM Crawford marched at the head of 400 militia into the Ohio Country to quell the Indians. He was fifty, the same age as his fellow-Virginian and lifelong friend, George Washington, who had asked him to undertake the expedition. Crawford was an experienced veteran in warfare and had had several encounters with the Indians. He had been in Ohio before, the first time as a lad with Washington on a surveying trip. Now he came reluctantly, for he had hoped to spend the rest of his days in peace on his estate. He was confident that he could quiet the Indian trouble. But the Indians were aroused and bitter from the brutal slaughter of their race by whites at Gnadenhutten, and they outsmarted Crawford's forces three miles north of today's Upper Sandusky. Crawford was captured, tied to a fifteen-foot stake and slowly burned to death from a fire of hickory logs kindled at his feet. One of Crawford's companions, Doctor Knight, was also captured but he escaped to recount the story for posterity. All through this county are Crawford statues and markers, and lore about the martyrdom. The tragedy happened in 1782 and has been the subject of many novels, including one by the Ohioan Zane Grey.

Upper Sandusky, the county seat, is at the upper end of the Sandusky River. Though it is in one sense a young town, having been laid out in 1843, its history starts long before. William Henry Harrison had a fort here in 1812 and some of his men are buried on the courthouse lawn. In a treaty, Wyandots were given a reservation, and remained until the city's founding. They are buried in the Indian cemetery, where today there is a replica of an Indian mission built in 1821 by the first Methodist missionary to the Indians, the great Reverend James B. Finley. The way was prepared for Finley by a mulatto, James Stewart, who came here in 1816. Finley's was the first Methodist mission in the Mississippi Valley.

Wyandot County. The shrine of Our Lady of Consolation at Carey.

Charles Dickens comments tartly in his uncomplimentary *American Notes* about his visit here in 1842. He and his wife "spent a troubled night in a large ghostly room with doors that lacked fastenings, both opening on the wild country whenever the wind blew."

Discarded crutches, wheelchairs and braces around the altar of a little frame church and a miraculous statue of the Virgin in a larger and newer brick church proclaim Carey as a city of cures. The churches are side by side, both called the Lady of Consolation. The newer Romanesque-Byzantine brick one has a carillon tower, exquisite stained-glass windows and a vaulted dome. The 36-inch statue of Mary with the Christ Child, a replica of a seventeenth-century miracle image, was fashioned in Luxembourg and installed in the old Ohio church in 1875. As many as 30,000 are present for certain holy days when the statue is carried aloft on a litter. Tradition has it that on such days it seldom rains, but if rain does come, not a drop falls on the image. A travelers' hospice, Pilgrim House, with fifty rooms presided over by brown-habited sisters of St. Francis, welcomes wayfarers of all faiths.

CRAWFORD COUNTY, 1815

Named for Colonel William Crawford

JOLLY old Colonel Kilbourne liked to come back to visit with his cronies in Bucyrus which he had surveyed and named in his youth. He often "made a night of it," singing and telling stories about how he picked the odd name in honor of his boyhood hero, the Persian general Cyrus, adding "bu" as a prefix for "beautiful." "For it is a beautiful spot," he always added. He was so enamored of the town that he wrote an eight-stanza poem in praise of it.

It is said only two other places have the same name, one in Kansas and the other in South Dakota, both settled by Ohioans and named for the town in their state. At any rate, the frequent pioneer confusion over towns with duplicate names was avoided in this one which became the county seat. With traffic of the nation whizzing in and

Crawford County. Railroad roundhouse at Crestline, busy railroad center.

out its big central square from all directions, it is hard to think that for many years the settlement's only outlet was an ox-team trail to Sandusky. This trip through virgin forests and wild country took two weeks. The pike, finished in 1834, connected Kilbourne's home in Worthington with Bucyrus and changed all this. When complete, it was the most important highway in the state, much of its route traversing the old Scioto Indian trail from Portsmouth to Upper Sandusky.

Bucyrus is a trade center for surrounding rural communities. It also has a number of small manufacturing concerns, one of which turns out post boxes that stand on street corners in metropolitan cities throughout the country.

Colonel William Crawford, captured by the Indians here, had the presence of mind to take off his sword, break it and drop it into a creek to prevent the savages from using it against him. The stream ever since has been known as Broken Sword Creek, and the little settlement nearby is called by the same name. What was claimed to be the identical sword was dug up in 1889 by a resident while planting corn on the bank of the creek. It had a gold pommel shaped into an eagle's head, such as a Revolutionary War army officer would carry. Buried beside it were several pieces of a broken blade.

Railroads put Crestline on the map and have kept it there. The city of 4,500 is an important transfer point for east and west passengers, crews and freight shipments. The ground shakes and buildings tremble with the rumble of long trains passing. But no one objects, for railroading is the city's livelihood. In the Crawford County Historical Museum on the top floor of the old city hall are relics of early trains and an interesting panorama of the town's beginnings. The original village was Livingston, from the family of that name who were feudal lords along the Hudson River. When the first railroad lines were laid a half-mile away, Livingston languished and the upstart settlement on the crest took Crestline for its name. The community grew rapidly when the New York Central and Pennsylvania railroads built their enormous round houses and car shops there.

Galion is twice as large as Crestline, and one of Ohio's fast growing centers. Large expensive homes set amidst landscaped acres in the expanding residential district attest to the new wealth created by railroad repair shops, the manufacture of telephone instruments, hydraulic hoists, heavy road machinery, burial vaults and other products.

MARION COUNTY, 1823

Named for General Francis Marion, a Revolutionary War Officer from South Carolina

MARION's giant earth-moving machines helped dig the Panama Canal and Boulder Dam. Most of the bumps and humps in construction of modern highways are smoothed by road rollers and tractors from this bustling city of 33,000 which takes its name from the county. Made by the Marion Steam Shovel Company and the Huber Manufacturing Company, they literally carry Marion's name around the world. Ohio, with a number of other

Marion County. Harding locking up a page of his paper, *The Marion Star.*

factories making similar, powerful equipment like power shovels, bulldozers and tractors of all kinds, sends such products to excavate the earth in the far parts of the globe.

The shovel and a bit of vigorous digging gave Marion its start. The story goes that one Jacob Foos, arriving after a long journey from the north, was thirsty from a steady diet of salt pork. Searching for good drinking water, he carved out a rough wooden spade, dug a hole and came upon abundant water. His grateful companions immediately said: "Let's call this place Jacob's Well." And Jacob's Well it became, even after it was selected as the county seat. Later it was given the more dignified name of Marion.

Marion is proud not only of its world-renowned digging and road-making machines, but also of the fact that the city became the home of the twenty-ninth president of the United States, Warren Gamaliel Harding, born in Blooming Grove (then Corsica), Morrow County.

Whatever appraisal the rest of the country places on Warren Harding, Marion reveres his memory with an almost religious fervor. Residents like to tell how he worked his way through Ohio Central College, now extinct, in Iberia; how, at nineteen, he came to Marion to work on the Marion *Star*. With little capital and inadequate equipment, he tackled the almost lifeless newspaper, changing its policy to Republican despite the predominatingly Democratic community. By a combination of excellent editorial writing and sound business methods he built it into a great newspaper, which he bought when he was twenty-one and owned until shortly before his death.

Despite corruption charges against some of his cabinet during Harding's administration, Marion friends stood by him, giving him their constant devotion. Harding himself was untouched by graft, they remind the world. Marion points to the able men in his cabinet like Charles Evans Hughes, Herbert Hoover and Andrew Mellon, secretaries of state, commerce and the treasury; to the Harding administration's accomplishments including the Limitation of Arms Pact of 1921, his government budget system and opposition to liquor interest. Harding is still Marion's hero. The city's $3 million high school, built in 1952 and one of the finest in the state, is named Harding High School as was the former high school, now a junior high. The Harding home on Mount Vernon Avenue is a public museum where mementoes of the Hardings are reverently displayed. The Harding mausoleum was built in Marion with money contributed from all parts of the country. The glistening white marble building is set dramatically amidst 10 acres of landscaped grounds, and is one of the most magnificent monuments erected to an American president.

VII
The Virginia Military District

INTRODUCTION

THE Virginia Military District consisted of 4,000,000 acres in southwestern Ohio between the Scioto and Little Miami Rivers, bounded on the south by the Ohio River and on the north by Auglaize, Hardin and Marion Counties.

Based on original charters granted in 1606 and 1609 by King James I of England, and also as the result of the George Rogers Clark Expedition of 1779, Virginia claimed a vague and vast sweep of western lands extending from "sea to sea." During the Revolutionary War each colony used whatever inducement it could to promote troop enlistments. Virginia, as early as the French and Indian Wars of the 1750s, had offered land in payment for military service; during the Revolution the same pattern was followed. However, since the colonies had united for the freedom and benefit of all, at the close of the war it was felt that those owning western lands should cede them to the government for the common good. When the Continental Congress made such a request in 1780, Virginia, eager to have her frontier settled by English-speaking people, led the states in complying. But she lacked enough good land to the southeast of the Ohio River to satisfy the bounty warrants she already had promised her sizable army and navy (she had more than twenty vessels). She asked, therefore, to be allowed to keep the tract between the Scioto and Little Miami. This was granted, and title to these acres was vested in the United States in trust for officers and enlisted men of Virginia.

In 1783 the Virginia legislature appointed a board of twenty army officers to handle the surveys and appropriation of bounty lands. The district land office was opened first in Louisville, Kentucky, and later moved to Chillicothe. The principal surveyor, General R. C. Anderson, employed a twenty-seven-year-old Virginian, Nathaniel Massie, as his assistant. In 1791 Massie made the first settlement within the district at Manchester on the Ohio River, and became a large land-owner. Townships were not surveyed in any regular form. Veterans or their heirs holding military land warrants located largely where they pleased. Consequently there was more confusion over titles than in any other part of the state. Virginians came in steady streams of colonizing and the stamp of that state and the gentle touch of the South spread throughout this section of Ohio.

LOGAN COUNTY, 1817

Named for General Benjamin Logan, Kentuckian who fought the Indians in the Mad River Valley in 1786

FROM the Sloans' little cabin, sure as springtime, would come the pungent odor of "Doc's" liniment boiling on the kitchen stove. The family lived in Zanesfield, named for Isaac Zane, who owned 1,800 acres in the beautiful Mad River Valley and lived there with his Indian wife. The hamlet was also the home of Simon Kenton in his last years. All that was long before the Sloans came. Doc Sloan, a harness maker, had a way with horses, and spent about as much time caring for ailing animals as in mending saddles and whiffletrees. He had learned about his brown, strong-smelling concoction from the Indians. It was in great demand when the first spring plowing stiffened horses' shoulders.

The Sloans were poor and the children had little chance for education. One of the boys, Earl, liked to read. One day Earl asked to borrow a book from a neighbor who operated a small private library. The man, looking over the boy's ragged clothes and rather dirty hands, said he couldn't trust one of his books to such an untidy fellow. Earl never forgot the incident. He vowed that when he grew up he would make a lot of money and buy all the books he wanted. Among the many stories in Zanesfield about Earl Sloan, one is that after selling his father's medicine in the neighborhood for a time, he and his brother Foreman left home to seek their fortune. They tied their shoes about their necks to save wear and carried a few jugs of the potion in their hands, and the recipe in their heads.

It was at the close of the Civil War, the heyday of the horse. They peddled their remedy from farm to farm, moved with the caravans of pioneers heading westward and followed the horse fairs. Soon they had their own horse and wagon. Earl, the leader in the venture, excitedly reported one day: "A fellow just told me he rubbed some of Pa's liniment on his back and it worked fine. Now I'm going to hawk it as good for man and beast!" He sold twice as much. Earl risked an advertisement in Chicago streetcars, and orders poured in. The brother seems to have dropped out, but Earl persevered, took his father's title of "doctor" and organized a company to manufacture the remedy.

In 1914 Earl Sloan built a $25,000 library endowed for $40,000 in his native Zanesfield, village of two hundred. He made sure that any Zanesfield boy who wanted a book could have one. Over the door is carved "Dr. Sloan's Library," with a medallion portrait of the donor, mustache and all, like his pictures on the liniment bottles. A huge boulder in the center of the village is inscribed to the memory of Kenton and Zane. But Sloan, who did more for the community than either of the other two, is ignored, like so many who contribute to our heritage.

When Sloan died in 1923, he left his million-and-a-half-dollar estate to the boys and girls of Logan County. As the result of his bequests the high school at Bellefontaine, the county seat, has an up-to-date vocational training department called the Sloan Industrial School. Another Sloan fund was established to help the city's youth who otherwise could not attend high school. Dr. Earl S. Sloan's liniment is still distributed, labeled now for humans only.

Bellefontaine, French for "beautiful fountain," was so named because of the numerous springs. It is on the site of an Indian village. This is the highest point in Ohio, 1,550 feet above sea level. The first concrete pavement in the United States was laid around the courthouse in 1891 and is still in use.

Logan County. Log cabin home of Isaac Zane, at Zanesfield.

Every little hollow and hillock in the surrounding countryside has its Indian tales. Near West Liberty, where Mac-o-chee Creek winds like a silvery eel through the lush valley, Kenton ran an Indian gantlet, and General Logan marched up from Kentucky to obliterate the Shawnee villages. This is the land of Ohio castles, two of them built after the Civil War by members of the distinguished Piatt family. Of French Huguenot origin, their antecedents settled on extensive military land grants here following the Revolutionary War in which one served on Washington's staff. James Whitcomb Riley is said to have composed his frost-is-on-the-pumpkin poem while a guest of the Piatts. The ceiling of the forty-foot drawing room in one of the castles was decorated with cupids and bow knots by a mural artist, especially brought from France for the work.

UNION COUNTY, 1820

So-named because it was formed from parts of surrounding counties

"I KNOW Marysville gets a lot of attention because of its beautiful lawns and trees," said a local newspaper editor. "But what is really outstanding in this village and in Union County is the community spirit. We are really a union county. Take our new county Memorial Hospital as an example. It's the only one in the county, and as modern and efficient a small hospital as there is anywhere in the United States." He went on to explain that when completed in 1952 its cost was over $600,000, a large sum to have been raised by a county with only a little more than 20,000 population. Everyone backed it, private citizens and public officials alike, and all practicing physicians in the county are on its staff. The one-story building, of contemporary design, is in Marysville, on a 12-acre plot surrounded by magnificent oak, hickory and dogwood trees.

Another community project is the big municipal swimming pool at Marysville Legion Park. The attractive high school in the village is surrounded by a velvety greensward which carries no "Please keep off the grass" signs. Such warnings are not needed, for students respect the grass, knowing it is maintained as another gesture of friendly cooperation by a local grass seed company. There are bigger businesses than this plant in Marysville: the Swiss-owned canned milk company and the factory making hardware and plumbing supplies. But the grass seed firm is the oldest and Marysville's own. It is the outgrowth of a modest hardware and seed store started in the 1870s by O. M. Scott, father of the present owner. Grass seed from New Zealand, Czechoslovakia, Denmark, Oregon and Kentucky is cleaned, blended and shipped to homeowners in all parts of the country.

Marysville, the county seat, was named for the daughter of Samuel Cuthbertson who founded the village in 1820. Three county fairs are staged annually: one in Marysville, one in Richwood to the north and the third in Plain City to the south.

In the latter part of the last century the busiest place in the county

Union County. County courthouse at Marysville, an example of the ornate courthouses built in Ohio during the latter part of the nineteenth century.

was Magnetic Springs. Rigs and carryalls from far and near brought invalids hoping to benefit from the mineral waters. The waters were discovered when a farmer, drilling for a well, struck a spring that gushed up many feet in the air like a fountain. The water had a peculiar magnetic quality so powerful that local tradition claims a knife blade immersed for a few minutes became sufficiently charged to pick up a pound of nails.

Union County, for generations a Republican stronghold, entered politics in a big way in the 1840 presidential campaign of William Henry Harrison. A county resident made a miniature log cabin for a wagon float in Harrison's big political parade. Otway Curry of Marysville wrote the Log Cabin song and played its accompaniment on his flute while sitting beside the cabin as Harrison's procession wound through Ohio. The song helped win the election for Harrison, the first "log cabin president."

Union County's occupation is agriculture; dairying and hog raising its specialties. A high percentage of the farms, which average over 100 acres each, are home-owned and managed with few tenant operators.

CHAMPAIGN COUNTY, 1805

Champaign, meaning open level country

COLONEL William Ward, a Virginian who in 1805 laid out Urbana, derived the name from the word "urban." His grandson, John Quincy Adams Ward, was to become Ohio's greatest sculptor. His best known work, a colossal bronze of Washington, stands at the subtreasury building in New York City where the president took his first oath of office. Several other Ward statues are in Central Park, among them the Indian Hunter, a replica of which his widow erected at the sculptor's grave in Urbana's Oakdale Cemetery.

Quincy Ward was inspired, he said, by a head of Apollo, the first sculpture he ever saw, in the home of a neighbor, Colonel John H. James. Like Ward's grandfather James had come from Virginia, and had participated in all the important doings of his adopted state. The gracious home he built in the 1830s once commanded an estate of many acres, but it is ringed now and made smaller by the expanding city. Through the James family's support of the Swedenborgian Church, Urbana became the Midwest center of this faith, and Urbana University was established by this sect. Now a junior college, and the only one in Ohio maintained separately, Urbana University is coeducational, with an enrollment of fifty and a faculty of ten. Part of its campus near the Mad River was a campsite for General Hull during the War of 1812, and later was Colonel James' gift to the college.

Urbana, the county seat, lies in the midst of a fertile agricultural section of large farms. The city, a trade center for this rich county, also developed several industries with the coming of three railroads in the latter part of the century. In the library, one of the earliest in Ohio, are mementoes of the Urbanan Brand Whitlock, novelist, re-

Champaign County. The square in Urbana, showing the Civil War monument.

form mayor of Toledo and distinguished ambassador to Belgium. General Robert L. Eichelberger, prominent in World War II, was born in Urbana.

At the northern edge of the county are the Ohio Caverns where stalactites and stalagmites decorate the highly colored walls and ceilings.

In a neglected little cemetery at a crossroads called Heathtown is the grave of the man who knew George Washington best, his Negro valet, Richard Stanhope. He was with his master from the Revolutionary War until he stood beside his deathbed. Washington's will gave him his freedom and 400 acres of land in the Virginia Military Tract in this county. Here he lived until his death in 1862 at the age of 114, according to his family. His descendants live in Urbana today.

FAYETTE COUNTY, 1810

The name a shortened version of Lafayette

LONG lines of lowing cattle and bleating sheep crowded the streets of Washington Court House in the early days. The animals kicked up dust, while the shouts and curses of drovers rang out continually. Today the city is still a live-stock center, and there is a big stockyard at the edge of town where cattle arrive by truck and train. They count the cattle, sheep and hogs handled annually by the million, and the business touches a $15 million figure. The region is given to ranchlike farms, many well over 1,000 acres. In the luxuriant pastures aristocratic red-brown Hereford cattle graze serenely. Signs proclaim Fayette County the "Hereford-shire of Ohio." Sheep in great numbers add their artistic touch to the scenery. There are all kinds of hogs, some of them calico-colored, for all the world like spotted china toy banks come alive and grown gigantic.

People in this part of Ohio are interested in horses, both racing and saddle stock. Probably more people ride and train horses than in any other county. The racing program at the County Fair, held in July, is an important feature. This devotion to the horse is a direct in-heritance from Virginia forefathers. The stamp of Virginia is ap-parent everywhere. Land here is said to have been given originally to

Fayette County. Fayette County is noted for its stock raising.

a Virginia regiment, with the stipulation that the county be named for Lafayette.

City fathers had added "Court House" to the name to distinguish it from other towns in Ohio called Washington. This is another Virginia touch, as the appendage "court house" is common in that state. The nearly 11,000 citizens of this city are proud of its name and usually refer to it as "Washington C.H." Woe to the visitor who leaves off those letters "C.H."!

Topping the great dome of the ornate courthouse is a graceful female figure, Astraea, Star Maiden, hobnobbing with the clouds. Her presence may be of small concern to the practical-minded stock breeders and manufacturers hurrying about in the streets below her. But she is the symbol of the county seat and can be seen for miles by travelers from whatever direction they come.

MADISON COUNTY, 1810

Named for James Madison

MADISON COUNTY is the land of big farms, some of the biggest in the state. A farm of 5,000 acres is not unusual and there are many of 2,000 and 3,000 acres. A motorist can drive for miles over the good roads of this level country and the entire time be skirting the boundary of only a single farm. A high percentage is under absentee ownership, operated by tenants. Often a resident manager, functioning like a corporation executive, is in charge; or the acres are handled by a farm management company, two of which have offices in London, the county seat. Such organizations are staffed by well trained agronomists prepared to take full responsibility from planting to harvest, make all purchases whether for a hoe or a hundred hogs, sell the produce, keep complete records and guarantee profits for owners. The most extensive holdings are those of a Columbus newspaper family whose land is in parcels in various sections of the county, the units covering several thousand acres. One of the largest farms, Orleton House, is in the northern part of the county.

Madison County. Air view of the London State Prison Farm on the outskirts of London.

It covers nearly 5,000 acres owned by a Cincinnati woman and has nearly thirty permanent tenants.

These large-scale operations are carried on with up-to-date machinery. Supervisors in jeeps ride from fields to pastures over miles of roads laid out within the farms. Horses, except saddle horses kept for pleasure, are practically nonexistent. Frequent sights on county highways are combines, tractors, corn pickers and trucks moving from one farm to another. Madison County's gross annual farm income in 1950 was $15,300,000; the principal source is hogs, 44 per cent of the total agricultural product. More than 76,000 acres were planted in corn in 1950.

In the southeast corner of the county, around Mount Sterling, is a different community pattern. Farms are small—less than 100 acres— and are family owned and managed. They are the outgrowth of a government resettlement project during the depression when 100 distressed farms in this and adjoining counties were purchased, subdivided and allotted to farmers facing relief. A simple six-room house, a barn and a poultry shed were built on each farm, and money was loaned for stock and equipment as a start. The long-term amortization plan enabled farmers eventually to own the properties. The local Farm

Home Administration director, in Madison County a trained agriculturist, supervises each farm program, with the result that 37 of Madison County's 44 farms in this category now are owned outright by families living there. The gross income per farm for 1950 was $6,300.

London, a town of 5,300 which dates from 1811, has some vigorous industries, such as factories making steel wool, automobile radiators and parts for farm machinery. Near London is the state prison farm of several thousand acres where prisoners with good behavior records are transferred from the Ohio Penitentiary at Columbus.

North of London is Lafayette, founded by William Minter, a Revolutionary War veteran who took up a 6,000-acre military grant. After the National Road was laid through the village, the Red Brick Tavern was built in 1837 and became a popular stagecoach stop. In the fine old building, which is still in use, the elegant Martin Van Buren drank tea, and William Henry Harrison and Henry Clay stopped there, too.

CLINTON COUNTY, 1810

Named for George Clinton of New York, vice president under James Madison and early advocate of the Erie Canal

WILMINGTON COLLEGE needed a dormitory for men, but lacked sufficient funds. The 500 students decided to build it themselves. The result was a cooperative work-and-study project unique in American college annals. A charming modern building, Marble Hall, named for the college president, was erected in 1951. The college takes its name from Wilmington where it is located, a city of 7,500 and the county seat. It is Ohio's only college under the Society of Friends. In a real sense college and city symbolize the county. Quakers arrived early and put their stamp on the district. Vexed by the South's growing slave labor, they left Virginia and the Carolinas.

Typical of the early architecture is the stagecoach tavern built in the 1820s on Snow Hill on the edge of town, now home of Wil-

Clinton County. College Hall, Wilmington College's "main building" begun in 1866 when the campus was known as Franklin College, was the first instance of self-help by Wilmington College students. Bricks were molded and burned in a kiln on campus and students aided with the rough construction.

mington's scenic country club. The Friends' Church, programmed and with a paid ministry, in contrast to the older "silent gathering," is the third largest Quaker meeting in the United States. Clinton County's gently rolling hills and rich bottom lands are watered by tributaries of the Little Miami such as Jonah's Run and Caesar's Creek, the latter named for a favorite Negro servant of an early surveyor. From the fact that the district holds national agricultural records comes the county's boast of being the "Garden Spot of the United States."

In addition to agriculture and education, Wilmington's development has included several industrial plants, among them one of the largest factories making wood-boring tools in the world, and a bridge company.

Denver is an important name; the first of the Denver family was a Revolutionary veteran who came in the early days from Virginia to take up military bounty lands. A landscaped city park of 60 acres with picnic and sports areas, it is a memorial to a scion of the family, twenty-three-year-old J. W. Denver Williams, Jr., a Marine corporal killed at Okinawa. Denver, Colorado, is also named for one of this family who emigrated to the west.

Sabina has been the center of Methodism since the 1890s when a large acreage here was developed as a Methodist State Conference Grounds for yearly meetings attended by hundreds of laity and ministers.

HIGHLAND COUNTY, 1805

Named for the high lands within its borders

A LITTLE flurry of snow powdered the housetops of Hillsboro the day before Christmas 1873. Suddenly the cold stillness was invaded by the high sweet voices of women, a great troupe of them, singing a hymn: "Give to the winds thy fears. . . ." Seventy women, social leaders of the conservative town, marched two

Highland County. A group of Hillsboro's prominent members of the Women's Christian Temperance Union, 1873.

abreast from the Presbyterian Church straight to the first of Hillsboro's thirteen saloons. Eliza Jane Thompson, sheltered daughter of an Ohio governor, wife of a judge, led them past the astonished bar keeper and his gaping customers. Lifting her trailing skirts, dodging the shiny brass spittoons, she knelt on the sawdust floor. Her followers, like herself trembling at their "immodesty," resolutely added their prayers to hers. Mrs. Thompson arose and explained to the bewildered saloon owner that the visit would be repeated until he closed his place. The women adjusted their stylish bonnets and departed to tackle the next saloon. Mrs. Thompson was forever after "Mother" Thompson. "Mother" was the invariable designation of the pioneer career woman, and Eliza Thompson was launched now on a life career. She had started one of the most astonishing and far-reaching movements in Ohio's history, the Women's Temperance Crusade. One by one Hillsboro's dispensing bars closed in despair, except that of one druggist. When the women erected a tent at his front door for continual prayers and hymn singing, he sued them for interfering with his business. The case dragged on, and finally he won a $5 judgment against them.

It was Dr. Dio Lewis' talk on liquor's evils that had touched off the Hillsboro women, many of whom were battling with the drink habit among their men folk. They took it as a religious mission, "the Whirlwind of the Lord." It spread until almost every town in southern Ohio had its band of Crusaders. One month after Mother Thompson's first prayer, more than 100 saloons in 25 Ohio towns were closed. The next year the world-wide Women's Christian Temperance Union was formed with the white bow-knot ribbon as its symbol.

Mother Thompson's home, a delightful yellow brick colonial now occupied by one of her heirs, was built by her father, Governor Allen Trimble, and is a venerated shrine of Hillsboro.

Early settlers were from Virginia, Maryland and Pennsylvania. Among the numerous fine old buildings is the county courthouse with massive classic pillars leading to a domed belfry, and roof bristling with chimneys from the many fireplaces. Hillsboro, like Rome a city built on seven hills, is the county seat. Along with several other industries the town has a bell foundry and farm machinery plant operated today by Miss Virginia Bell, granddaughter of the man who established it nearly a century ago.

A Mound Builders relic is well-preserved Fort Hill, southeast of Hillsboro. A 50-acre tract of land, dense with fine old trees, is enclosed by weathered limestone walls, some 25 feet thick. One of the first to study it was Edwin H. Davis, born in Hillsboro in 1811.

In Rainsboro to the east, harness races used to attract thousands. The place is also famous as the home of the outlaw Robert McKimie, the Jesse James of Ohio of the 1880s. After several attempts at reform McKimie resumed his old ways. He spent the end of his life hiding from the law in one of the numerous caves in the scenic gorge of Paint Creek's Rocky Fork.

Greenfield, founded by General Duncan McArthur, Chillicothean and an Ohio governor, was named by him for its flat green plains. One of Ohio's finest school plants is located here, the Edward Lee McClain High School, vocational building and elementary school on a 14-acre landscaped campus. Valued at several millions, the school was given to the town by McClain who made his fortune from a special horse collar and pad.

Leesburg was settled by Quakers and named for the Lee family of Virginia.

Among the famous sons of the county are Albert J. Beveridge, biographer; numerous Beechers related to Henry Ward Beecher and his sister Harriet Beecher Stowe; comic-strip artist Milton A. Caniff; Dr. Frank C. Hibben, archaeologist, and Dr. Samuel G. Hibben, lighting expert.

BROWN COUNTY, 1817

Named for General Jacob Brown, officer of the War of 1812, a Pennsylvania Quaker

"SEE THAT light twinkling across the river? That's in the Reverend Rankin's house at Ripley. Liberty Hill they calls it. He helps the likes of you. You and the young un'll be safe all right if you git there." The nervous Negro woman, Eliza

Harris, standing on the Kentucky bank of the Ohio River, held her baby tight to her bosom as she listened to the rough riverman. He was just drunk enough to risk helping a runaway slave. It was a March night and bitter cold. The ice in the river, half a mile wide here, was breaking up. Eliza looked with terror at those slippery ice floes. How could she stand on them? But anything, even death for herself and child in the frigid water, was better than going back to her mistress. She stepped off, slipped and slid, fell, regained her footing, slipped again. Soon her clothes were soaking and beginning to freeze to her skin. But she kept on. The blinking light was getting nearer, nearer. At last she scrambled up the bank and staggered around to the kitchen door of the house. Mrs. Rankin, the minister's wife, took her in and gave her food and fresh clothes for herself and her baby. But Eliza had to leave that very night. One of the Rankins' sons saddled a horse and stealthily took Eliza and her child on to the north to other Underground Railroad operators. Inching secretly north from "station" to "station" she was reunited with her husband and reached freedom in Sandusky.

The following October the Cincinnati Synod of the Presbyterian Church met at Ripley. Harriet Beecher and her father, Reverend Lyman Beecher, head of Cincinnati's Lane Seminary, were among the attenders, and stayed with the Rankins. Square-jawed John Rankin strolled with his guests to the picket fence edging his lawn and recounted his experiences in helping escaping slaves, especially Eliza. Slim, serious-minded Harriet used the story later in *Uncle Tom's Cabin* and made it one of Ohio's immortal tales. At the Rankin house at this time Harriet was introduced to another guest, the Biblical scholar Calvin Stowe, a recent widower, who a little more than a year later became her husband.

John Rankin, along with Levi Coffin of Cincinnati, was the leading backer of the Underground Railroad in Ohio. The Rankin house was placed strategically on the river where it was easily accessible to slaves fleeing from the south. Rankin's wife, nine sons and four daughters made a devoted assisting army. They cared for more than 2,000 fugitives, whose value as then estimated was over a million dollars. In 1939 the Rankin home became the property of the Ohio State Archaeological and Historical Society which maintains it as a public museum.

Brown County. John Rankin House at Ripley, a station on the Underground Railroad.

Of late, Ripley has become the center for large-scale leather goods manufacturing in plants employing several hundred workers. Factories here make shoes, and also harnesses and packs for United States Air Force parachutes.

Georgetown, the county seat, is an attractive town famed as the boyhood home of General Ulysses S. Grant. The house where he grew up was on a street now named Grant Avenue. It was built in 1823 by his father, Jesse, who had a tannery nearby. Though Grant was not enthusiastic about school, the schoolhouse he attended has become a much-visited American memorial, housing battle flags of his Civil War engagements and other mementoes. During Grant's boyhood the leading citizen was wealthy Thomas L. Hamer through whom Grant obtained appointment to West Point. A Brown County village to the north, Hamersville, is named for Hamer.

PIKE COUNTY, 1815

Named for Zebulon Pike, discoverer of Pike's Peak

WAVERLY was at fever heat. The canal was coming here instead of to Piketon! Robert Lucas, member of the legislature, and James Emmitt, leading citizen, had influenced the route change. Both owned large tracts of land around Waverly, the town that took its name from Scott's Waverly novels. Many difficulties beset the canal's construction. Insects from the swamps spread sickness among the laborers. The terrain resisted the primitive digging methods. It was 1832 before the ditch reached Waverly. And then there was no water in it! The gravel in the bed let it leak away. At last a certain September day was set as the time when water could be expected. The entire populace lined the banks. To their amazement there was still not a trickle in the long straight cut. The crowd waited, growing more impatient by the hour. Just as everyone was about to give up and go home, a great shout was raised. Water! Water! In an hour or two there was enough of a flow to bring a boat with dignitaries from Chillicothe. With the canal Waverly became an exchange port and grew to two or three thousand population.

Waverly in mid-summer 1952 was caught in the same kind of excitement again. This time it was because the village was selected as the site of a billion-dollar atomic plant. Another Oak Ridge was to be created in the winding valley where vestiges of the old canal still can be seen. The leisurely pattern of life along the Scioto was stirred as it had not been for more than a hundred years. After the passing of the canal, Waverly had quieted and shrunk to a population of 1,700. Now it would have to stretch its seams to take in an influx of about 30,000 workers needed in operations of the gigantic plant. To supply one essential alone, the electricity, a fifteen-company combine of electric power companies was organized in a $400 million program to build two steam-generating plants.

This time Piketon, a village of 800 to the south, will share in the prosperity, for the new activity is to spread along the Columbus-Portsmouth Pike in both directions from Waverly. Piketon, the county seat, was settled in 1814, fifteen years before Waverly. Intense rivalry developed between it and Waverly. Piketon lost the life-giving canal and languished. Hopes revived when several early railroads were planned through the county. But Waverly, to hang on to its canal business and keep industry from Piketon, blocked the roads. In 1861, in the final "battle" of the two-town "war," the county seat moved to Waverly.

Near Waverly is Lake White State Park, with a 350-acre lake surrounded by wooded hills and charming homesites. The lake was state-made in the 1930s at a cost of several million dollars.

In the hilly western part of the county is Pike State Park, a 7,500-acre primeval forest with Lake Pike, a "mountain lake," dropped between high untenanted hills. Leading to the park, skyline drives follow 150-year-old roads developed from buffalo and Indian trails. Signposts along them mark tiny crossroad settlements with such descriptive names as Hungry Holler, Plug Run, Windy Ridge, Buckskin Hill and Sulphur Lick.

When Waverly was growing rich and pert on canal trade, a scissors-grinder, August Hefner, got off a packet one day with his machine strapped to his back.

"Want to have your razor sharpened? I'll give it a fine edge for ten cents." He stopped the first man he met.

"No thanks—that's too much money."

The scissors-grinder became a familiar village figure, with the monotonous ringing of his bell proclaiming his craft. Housewives gave him their knives to sharpen and his business was good. He lived alone except for a mongrel dog, and had little contact with his fellows. When the man died in the 1870s, neighbors found he had bought a plot in the cemetery and had composed an epitaph. His tombstone, today a Waverly landmark, carries a carving of his grinding machine and his dog, together with the crude inscription he had written:

When your razor is dull and you want a shave
Think of the man that lives in this grave.
For there was a time
It might have been whet
But you was a-feared of a dime
And now it is too late

Pike County. The cave home of the hermit William Hewitt, south of Chillicothe on the Columbus-Portsmouth Pike. Workmen constructing the roadway built the marker in his memory.

Beside the pike north of Waverly is the cave where big William Hewitt, a Virginia aristocrat, lived as a hermit. Standing straight as a "silver-tipped lightning rod," he dressed in deerskins and moccasins, slept on pelts and spoke to no man. In the early 1800s, as a young man, he fled to the Ohio wilderness after quarreling over the disposition of the family estate. A marker erected by early road builders at the cave entrance reminds today's motorists of this strange frontier personality.

ADAMS COUNTY, 1799

Named for John Adams

YEARS before Columbus' time, a mysterious people, the first Ohioans, worked long and hard for many

175

Adams County. The Great Serpent Mound.

months on a bluff beside what is now called Brush Creek in Adams County. In some manner they cleared the ground on this flat elevation and moved tremendous quantities of earth, cleverly fashioning it into a gigantic serpent. For want of a better name we call these people the Mound Builders. When white settlers arrived, hundreds of years later, those earlier inhabitants had vanished, leaving behind, particularly in southern Ohio, hundreds of earthworks, embankments, walled enclosures, village sites and cemeteries. One of the most impressive is the Serpent Mound, lying coiled and still on this secluded spot, defying erosion through centuries of rain and wind. From jaw to tail tip it twists over a quarter of a mile, with the body averaging twenty feet in width. Authorities claim it is the largest effigy or image mound in the world. The Adams earthen serpent is generally believed to be a religious symbol. To many peoples, ancient and modern, the serpent has been an emblem of both good and evil. For some, its habit of shedding and renewing its skin has signified eternal life.

The Adams County mound, which is near the village of Loudon, was first explored by Frederick Putnam, a Boston scientist. He collected money in 1887 to purchase it and a surrounding plot of 60 acres, which he then gave to the Peabody Museum of Harvard University. In 1900 the museum deeded it to the Ohio State Archaelogical and Historical Society, by which it is now maintained as a state park.

Manchester, founded in 1791 by Nathaniel Massie on his way to Chillicothe, was the first settlement in the Virginia Military District, and the sixth town settled in Ohio. It is at a beautiful high bend in the Ohio in sight of several scenic islands in the river. In 1797 Massie built a handsome house at Buckeye Station near Manchester, commanding a fine view of the river. It was probably the first large house in the state. The town became an important change station for stagecoaches from Kentucky, and a steamboat embarkation point. For many years it was known for its pearl button factory which utilized the prolific mussel shells dragged from the Ohio River. In its early days Manchester tried to become the county seat, but lost to West Union because Massie and General Arthur St. Clair, territorial governor, were in opposite political camps.

ROSS COUNTY, 1798

Named for James Ross of Pennsylvania, a Federalist friend of Governor Arthur St. Clair

If Ohio was to be a state—and talk in Chillicothe in 1802 was about nothing else—there would have to be a state seal for official documents. William Creighton, though only twenty-one, was one of the committee appointed to design it. He saddled his horse and rode out to Thomas Worthington's estate, thinking Worthington might have some ideas for the seal. Thirty-three-year-old Worthington, a leader in political and social affairs, was living in a big log house while awaiting completion of his spacious stone villa, planned by his friend Benjamin Latrobe, architect of · Washington, D. C. Worthington called his place Adena, which he said meant "Paradise" in Persian. Today, carefully restored, it is state-owned and one of Ohio's showplaces.

Creighton got into a card game, played the night through and forgot all about the seal. Dawn broke. The sun, moving up behind the distant hill called Mount Logan, threw rosy, golden glows over wheat in the fertile plain. Creighton pointed to the scene unfolding below: "There's our seal, gentlemen," he said. The others, likewise impressed, agreed. The sketch which was adopted showed the sun behind the hills, with a sheaf of wheat in the foreground symbolizing the new state's abundance, and seventeen bunched arrows indicating Ohio would be the seventeenth state in the union. The seal now in use is again like the original, despite changes at various times which introduced a canal boat, a railroad car and even a blacksmith! Though 1803 is accepted as the official date of Ohio statehood, the imprint on the first seal was 1802. In the latter year the constitution was adopted. The first draft was written by the brilliant young Michael Baldwin, later first Speaker of the House. He used the top of a whisky barrel for a table in the rooms where the territorial legislature met above a gambling room and grog shop.

Soon there was a permanent territorial courthouse of stone, razed later to make way for the present classic county courthouse. A faithful replica of the first building houses the *Gazette,* heir of the *Scioto Gazette,* founded in 1800, one of the first newspapers in the Northwest Territory. Its editor, Nathaniel Willis, participated in the Boston Tea Party and learned his printer's trade from Benjamin Franklin.

Chillicothe was an exciting place. Only two years previously, in 1800, it had succeeded Cincinnati as capital of the Northwest Territory. Nathaniel Massie, carrying his surveyor's sextant and chains up the Scioto River, had founded the town at Paint Creek's falls in 1796, one of fourteen Ohio settlements to his credit. Chillicothe, the name he gave it, meant "town" in Indian language. Settlers were mostly Virginians, people of distinction, men of means who had in many cases bought the bounty rights of neighbors in this, Virginia's Military District. Above all, they were young. Massie at thirty-five was one of the oldest.

Edward Tiffin, a physician, married to Worthington's sister, brought his slaves to Ohio where he freed them though they continued in his employ. He was in his twenties when he came and carried with him a letter from his friend and Virginia neighbor, George Washington,

Ross County. Ohio's first state house, 1805, Chillicothe. An official replica by H. H. Bennett.

commending him to Governor St. Clair. The letter hangs in the Ross County Museum on Fifth Street, a treasure house of early Ohio relics. Tiffin, as speaker of the territorial legislature, led the agitation for statehood. Governor St. Clair, able soldier of the Revolution who had sacrificed his fortune for that cause, felt the settlers were not ready for the self-government which statehood implied. The controversy, one of progressive Republican ideas against conservative Federalism and of youth against age, grew bitter. Mobs invaded St. Clair's head-quarters. Stones were flung at him and he was saved from injury only by the intervention of Worthington. President Thomas Jefferson, sympathetic with Chillicothean aims, removed General St. Clair. Ohio became a state, the first carved from the vast Northwest Territory. Tiffin, elected governor without opposition, was inaugurated in March 1893. Worthington became one of Ohio's first two senators, later governor of the state. While governor he founded the Ohio State Library.

Ross County. Adena, home of Ohio's first governor, Thomas Worthington, before present-day restoration.

Chillicothe remained Ohio's capital, except for the Zanesville interval, 1810–1812, until the capital was removed permanently to Columbus.

The city, with a population now of 21,000, has been the county seat since the beginning. The cultivated settlers followed Worthington's example and built classic homes in the wilderness. They furnished them with carpets, silver and exquisite furniture carted with the greatest difficulty over the mountains. Many of the houses, like surrounding county farm estates, are lived in by descendants of the builders. Chillicothe as a result is a mecca for devotees of early American architecture.

Removal of the state capital was a blow, but Chillicothe rallied with the coming of the canal in the 1830s, an era of vigorous prosperity. On Kinnikinnick Creek (an Indian name for the tobacco mixture used in peace pipes) one of Ohio's first paper mills was started early in the 1800s. Papermaking is Chillicothe's leading industry today. The city is the home of Dard Hunter, world-famous authority on papermaking; the late John Bennett, author of *Master Skylark*; Burton Stevenson, prolific author and anthologist, renowned also as librarian who established camp libraries in World War I. The 2,155-bed U.S. Veterans Hospital, on the site of Camp Sherman of World War I, and the 1,600-acre Federal Reformatory are located at Chillicothe.

Southwestern Ross County in the Paint Creek Valley has some

of Ohio's finest scenery and is known as "Ohio's Wonderland." In wild country are the Seven Caves, some pushing 1,000 feet underground with vaulted cathedral-like walls. At Bainbridge is the first dental college in America, now a public museum.

PICKAWAY COUNTY, 1810

Name probably a phonetic rendering of Piqua, the name of an Indian tribe

ON A warm October day in 1774, Logan the Mingo chief was sitting under a sappling elm when the English militia man John Gibson came upon him. As a result of their meeting the tree became the most famous one in Ohio, known as the Logan Elm. Grown today to massive size, it is one of the oldest living things in the state. Ohio, so much younger than the elm, has laid out a little park around it, braced its aged limbs and planted the ground at its foot with monuments and plaques. It is a few miles south of Circleville, the county seat.

Gibson on that long-ago day had been searching for Logan since dawn and at once got on with his errand: "I was sent to find you. . . . They want you to sign the treaty with the other chiefs. . . . My commander, Lord Dunmore the Virginia governor, promises the Indians certain lands if there will be an end to bloodshed. They are all waiting for you at the camp." The camp, called Charlotte for the wife of King George III, was nearby. Its site is marked today.

Logan continued to sit in silence, fingering his gun, a weapon of the best English make, Gibson noted. Gibson knew Logan, heretofore the white man's friend, had been raiding in revenge for the slaying of his family by an irresponsible frontiersman. But he knew, too, that Dunmore felt no treaty would hold without the influential Logan's participation.

"I will not go to the white man's camp. I will agree to no treaty. I am a fighter, not a counselor for peace." Thus Logan broke his silence. Gibson was startled to see tears, rare in an Indian's eyes, come to Lo-

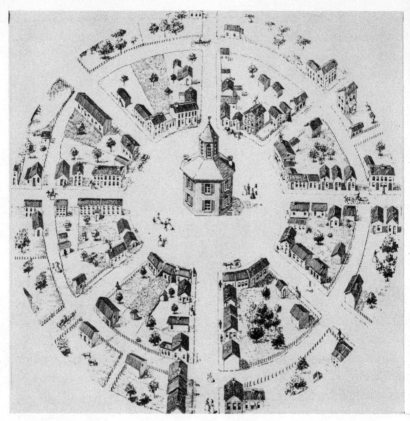

Pickaway County. Circleville, 1836. Drawing by G. F. Wintich.

gan's. The Mingo had learned the white man's language in his boyhood in Pennsylvania where his parents, on friendly terms with
William Penn, christened their boy Logan, along with his Indian
names, for James Logan, Penn's secretary. Gibson listened spellbound.
Grabbing a piece of paper from the buckskin pouch at his belt, he
hastily jotted down the words pouring from Logan's lips as he sat there
under the tree. When the scout returned to camp, Lord Dunmore
called in his staff to hear the message Gibson had transcribed:

"I appeal to any white man," Logan had begun, "to say if ever he
entered Logan's cabin hungry and he gave him not meat. If ever he
came cold and naked and he clothed him not. During the last long and
bloody war, Logan remained idle in his cabin, an advocate of peace.

I had even thought to live with you but one man last spring in cold blood murdered all the relatives of Logan, not even sparing my women and children. There runs not a drop of my blood in the veins of any living creature. This called on me for revenge. . . . I have killed many. I have fully glutted my vengeance. For my country I rejoice at the beams of peace. But who is there to mourn for Logan? Not one."

Dunmore reported the speech when he returned to Williamsburg. Thomas Jefferson printed it, giving it wide circulation. The other Indian leaders signed the peace without Logan. In a few months the American Revolution broke. Dunmore, the last royal governor of Virginia, fled for his life to a British ship and returned to England. His lordship's name is nearly forgotten, but Logan's speech has become an American classic. The elm lives, too, not only here but in numerous parks and schoolyards where little shoots from it have been planted reverently in Logan's memory. Logan's life was brief and sad after the peace he ignored. He wandered from village to village until he was killed by irresponsible whites as he sat in reverie by his lonely campfire.

The first Sunday in October the Ohio History Day Association meets under the gnarled branches of the old elm to honor Logan. The association was organized by the late Dr. and Mrs. Howard Jones of Circleville. Dr. Jones in 1886 completed an illustrated work on the nests and eggs of Ohio birds, a lifetime undertaking by members of his family.

When settlers came to Circleville in 1810 they found remains of a circular Mound Builder embankment within which they laid out their town, the county seat. An eight-sided courthouse was built within a round village green. The two main streets were platted as circles within the ancient curved wall, cross streets radiating out like spokes of a wheel. When the canal came through and the mounds were dug into, many bones and artifacts were discovered indicating this had been a populous town in prehistoric times. Citizens found the circled streets impractical and squared up their town in the 1840s. A distinguished early citizen, Cabel Atwater, backed public schools and canals, and in 1838 brought out the first history of Ohio.

Farms laid out eliptically, following the contour of the land, were settled by Virginians who built brick houses in the style of the South.

Pickaway County. The Logan Elm, under which the Mingo Chief Logan delivered his classic oration rejecting the white man's peace overtures.

Cornfields reach to the horizon. Blooded cattle graze in meadows marked off by miles of white fences. Circleville, in the midst of all this agricultural wealth, stages each October a colorful harvest festival known as the Pumpkin Show.

VIII The Hanging Rock Area

INTRODUCTION

DURING the early nineteenth century an area in southern Ohio and northern Kentucky became the center of pioneer iron-making. Nature had made accessible all the necessary ingredients for the industry: iron deposits in the hills; limestone and clay; forests for charcoal and, when the trees gave out, rich quantities of coal as substitute fuel. The Ohio River offered cheap transportation to markets. By the time the Civil War broke out there were more than sixty small furnaces. Because of an oddly formed projecting cliff beside the river, the district was known as the Hanging Rock Area.

LAWRENCE COUNTY, 1816

Named for James Lawrence, naval hero, remembered for his words, "Don't give up the ship"

HIS Negroes were well cared for, he knew, but John Means was convinced slavery was wrong. Unable to free his slaves in his native South Carolina, he left the South, and in 1819 moved into Ohio to liberate them. Means settled at a town called Hanging Rock for the high sandstone cliff which juts like a cornice over the river bank. A few years after his arrival, iron was

Lawrence County. Vesuvius Recreation Area north of Ironton and Hanging Rock.

discovered nearby, and Means set up a blast furnace, calling it Union Furnace, the first one north of the river. Others followed him, and by mid-century lands on both sides of the Ohio were dotted with vigorous little iron furnaces, and people spoke of it as the Hanging Rock Iron Region. The name became practically a trade designation.

The leading ironmaster was John Campbell, who came from Ripley. He is given credit for pioneering in the "hot blast" method, which revolutionized the industry. His furnace was Vesuvius. Each furnace had a name and was the core of a settlement with homes for workers, a church, stores and a school. The ironmaster was ruler of the domain. Campbell, a big, sternly dignified man, expanded his business to include coal mining and other interests. In 1849 he purchased a large tract near Hanging Rock, and founded a town to which he gave the appropriate name Ironton, now the county seat. Here was Big Etna Blast Furnace, largest in the world; the celebrated Hecla Furnace where car wheels for early railroads were cast, as well as such famous

Civil War guns as the "Swamp Angel" which pounded Confederates at Charleston Harbor. Because of its tough quality, local iron was in demand for heavy ordinance during the Civil War, and furnaces worked at capacity. Ironton flourished.

Local ore began to give out about the time Lake Superior ore, superior in quality and quantity, was coming in. Iron and steel mills were enticed north, nearer the lake ports to which the Michigan ore was shipped. One by one the old Hanging Rock furnaces were abandoned. Along the river today are their smoke stacks, steadily rusting away, the sturdy foundation stones in tumbled ruins. They are ghostly relics of an old order gone forever.

Ironton, after a slow decline, has revived. Now a city of 20,000, it is enjoying rapid expansion from diversified manufacturing, and is the center of a growing modern chemical industry. The American Chemical and Dye Corporation has a large plant near Ironton at South Point, practically the most southerly spot in Ohio. The village, heretofore, has been concerned chiefly with its apple orchards and its view, one of the famous sights in Ohio where both West Virginia and Kentucky shores can be seen. Three other giant chemical concerns have moved into the area, employing many workers, absorbing hundreds of valley acres and generally changing Lawrence County economy.

SCIOTO COUNTY, 1803

Named for the river, Indian word for deer

CELERON DE BIENVILLE and his retinue beached their canoes at the mouth of the Scioto. Against the wilderness setting the Frenchman looked oddly out of place in his resplendent uniform. It was 1749 at the site of today's Portsmouth, the county seat. Celeron found a well established Shawnee village, and was disturbed to note there were a good many English traders and scouts living here, too. He ordered the British to be gone, for they were encroaching on French possessions. They only laughed at him, whereupon Celeron signaled pompously to his followers and they moved off down the Ohio. But first he sank a lead plate in the mud

187

Scioto County. Shawnee State Forest.

of the river. It proclaimed the Ohio Country as belonging to his king, Louis XV. Celeron had been dropping these plates at strategic points all along the river, and some of them were found years later by boys playing along the shore.

In 1803 Portsmouth was founded. It was a natural place for a city. The Scioto River led north to inland settlements, while the Ohio brought trade from Pittsburgh to the Mississippi. Portsmouth's future was assured when it became the southern terminus for the Ohio Canal. Packets brought produce from the interior, carried back iron products from neighboring blast furnaces, bricks from Scioto County kilns and stone from quarries in the hills. Ohio River boats loaded and unloaded their cargo on the docks, and Portsmouth boomed. When the canal gave way to railroads, Portsmouth was lucky too, becoming a junction point for many roads. Again when local ore gave out, and charcoal furnaces disappeared, modern steel mills on both sides of the river took their place.

Today this city of 35,000, still the gateway to the rich Scioto Valley, is feeling the impact of a new way of life. It is only 20 miles from Waverly, picked in 1952 as the site of the colossal atomic energy plant which is revolutionizing the valley. Portsmouth is within the orbit of the Detroit Steel Company's expansion, including a blast furnace which the company claims will be the biggest in the world. The city's location, as always, is its greatest asset for it is accessible by rail and river barge to many markets.

In the 1790s Congress set aside over 35,000 acres in the southeastern corner of the county for French settlers who lost their lands around Gallipolis because of defective titles. Though only a few took up their claims, one French settlement developed and was named Burrsburgh for Aaron Burr. Later Massachusetts pioneers renamed it Haverhill for their home town.

The magnificent Shawnee Forest, largest of Ohio's state forests, is in this county. Along with a careful reforestation program, the beautiful country is being developed with campsites, good roads and picnic areas. It is well named the "Little Smokies of Ohio."

JACKSON COUNTY, 1816

Named for Andrew Jackson, hero of the Battle of New Orleans, fought just before the county was formed

ON A midsummer day in 1818 a raft zigzagged crazily on the Ohio River. Huddled aboard were thirty-five frightened Welsh men, women and children ringed about by their possessions. Pilots, poling desperately to keep the big craft afloat, managed to guide it into the harbor at Gallipolis, "Paris of the West." The weary voyagers were welcomed by the French residents who hurried to the levee to give a helping hand. The newcomers understood no French, and the French no Welsh. The travelers were able to make it clear, however, that they wanted to stop long enough to repair their leaking raft and to replenish food supplies. They would then continue to Paddy's Run near Cincinnati, where they were to join relatives. But they did not resume their journey, for their women folk revolted. That night terrific winds and rain whipped into the valley, carrying the raft downstream. Though it was recovered and was still usable, the Welsh women would have none of it. They recalled how they had embarked three months before from Liverpool on a sailing vessel which almost floundered in Atlantic gales, had made the exhausting trek from Baltimore overland to Pittsburgh, and worst of all, had come down the Ohio on the raft. Now, after last night's fearful storm, they determined to go no further.

Recognizing defeat, the Welsh men began to explore the country. They bought land to the north for $1.25 an acre—hilly land, but it reminded them of Wales. They got work on the new pike being laid from Gallipolis to Chillicothe, now Route 35. The Welsh, moving north along the road, settled in Jackson County, in the town of Jackson, picked as the county seat two years before; in Centerville, now called Thurman; to the west at Oak Hill; in numerous tiny communities in the hills.

Welsh was the language of the market place, the one-room schools, the log churches. The first boom came in 1830 when a Welsh minister, digging a water well in his dooryard in Jackson, struck a rich vein of coal. His fellow-countrymen knew what to do about this for many had been coal miners in their homeland. They sent for relatives and

Jackson County. The original Globe Furnace in Jackson, and some of the workers, photographed in 1872 shortly after it was started by Thomas T. Jones, early Ohio ironmaster.

friends. The Welsh invasion of Jackson County was under way. To-day's citizens are largely descendants of those first Welsh, and Welsh names are everywhere.

In the hills, the Welsh Hills some call them, nature hid precious wealth: salt, coal, limestone, iron, clay. From such lavish gifts of the earth the Welsh molded a pioneer empire of coal mining, iron foundries and brickmaking, all of them important today in the industrial structure of Ohio and of the nation.

Jackson, hilltop city of 7,000, is the center of the silvery iron industry of the United States. It is the only community where ironmaking, once so prevalent in this district, survives. Here are the Jackson Iron Company and the Globe Iron Company, the latter the world's largest producer of this metal of high silicon content used as a "mix" by malleable foundries and steel mills. The company is operated by great-grandsons of Thomas Jones, a Welshman, who one hundred years ago ran a blast furnace, now a tumbled ruins on man-made Lake Jackson. He was typical of pioneer iron mongers in this region. His furnace is said to have supplied iron plate for the battleship

Merrimac, later captured by the Confederates and used by them in the naval battle with the *Monitor* in 1862. Jones is buried in one of the county's many rural churchyards, where gravestone inscriptions are in Welsh.

Long before the Welsh came, well-padded paths led to the site of present-day Jackson. Buffalo and other wild animals, Indians and, later, white scouts, came for the salt in the springs. Daniel Boone, captured by the Indians, was forced to boil salt for them here until he managed to escape.

Wellston, to the northeast of Jackson, was built along Little Raccoon Creek by Harvey Wells who had a blast furnace here. By 1900 the city reached a census of almost 9,000, which has declined somewhat since the rich iron and coal deposits have run out. However it has a number of vigorous small industries and is an unusually attractive city.

VINTON COUNTY, 1850

Named for Samuel Vinton, prominent United States Congressman and Gallipolis lawyer

In Paris in 1856 a wealthy Pole, Peter Zaleski, leafed through a sheaf of papers from America. They were reports about rich ore deposits, coal veins and woodlands in a part of Ohio called Vinton County. Zaleski fingered the spot on his map. He was a banker and financial adviser to a little colony of wealthy Poles who had fled their native land and, like Zaleski, were living in France. He organized the Zaleski Mining Company, which bought many acres of Vinton County land. An agent laid out a town and called it Zaleski. He lined the streets with houses for workmen and built a "castle" for Zaleski who expected to emigrate. A furnace, called Hope Furnace, was built of massive rocks for smelting the ore. For a time the venture paid off, and Zaleski, an odd name on the Ohio map, was a busy place. Somehow the iron business failed. The little houses and the castle stood vacant, and the town shrunk within itself. Zaleski never visited it.

Vinton County. One of several ruins of early iron furnaces established by Peter Zaleski.

The town is the gateway today of Zaleski State Forest, an 18,000-acre scenic stretch containing Lake Hope State Park, named for the old furnace, now a picturesque ruin overrun with vines and wild growth. On the edge of the park is McArthur, trim county-seat village of 1,500 with a new courthouse. The town was named for Duncan McArthur, early Ohio governor.

Vinton's population in the 1950 census was 10,800, smallest of any county. Though it has declined numerically since 1910, renewed life is coming from the farm reclamation program directed by the State Agricultural Experiment Station and county agricultural agents. On the hilly land bad farming practices together with erosion played havoc with crop yields. The soil restoration plan, started in 1940, doubled harvests and farm income by 1950. A new day is dawning in Vinton County.

IX The Anthony Wayne Country

INTRODUCTION

GENERAL Anthony Wayne's decisive victory over the Indians in 1794 at Fallen Timbers near Maumee, and his peace pact the next year at Greenville, opened western Ohio and the vast northwest beyond to peaceful settlement. Two other generals, Josiah Harmar and Arthur St. Clair, had preceded him in unsuccessful attempts to quell the Ohio Indians. The three campaigns took the men and their armies through western Ohio from the Ohio River to Lake Erie. To develop a memorial to Wayne and the others in this part of Ohio, the state legislature in 1947 created the Anthony Wayne Parkway Board. The plan, as yet many years from completion, calls for making a unified parkway in the territory. No new highway is to be built. Instead, existing roads which follow or adjoin the three generals' military routes will be marked as the Anthony Wayne Parkway with signs bearing the silhouette of Wayne in tricorn hat and eighteenth-century uniform. These placards will guide modern motorists through this country so rich in historic lore. Already many of the markers are up. Work is going forward on roadside landscaping, restoration of historic sites, parks and recreation areas, involving a total of 60,000 acres.

Wayne's was one of the great achievements in American history. As western settlements increased, so did resistance by the Indians who fought to retain homelands and hunting grounds against white encroachment. Pioneers had been subjected continuously to murderous attacks. The Indians grew more menacing after they defeated Harmar in 1790 and St. Clair in 1791. The red men were further encouraged by the British who, in defiance of agreements at the close of the Revolutionary War, kept their fort at Detroit. George Washington, discouraged by the fate of the first two commanders, and desperate over the continued bloodshed in the west, picked Wayne to try for a third time to check the Indians and bring peace to the Ohio Country. Washington had some misgivings about Wayne, for, despite a distinguished career and unquestioned personal bravery, his recklessness in battle had earned him the title "Mad Anthony." Wayne, however, more than justified the President's confidence.

In the Greenville Treaty the Indians not only gave up a great part of what is now southwestern Ohio, but agreed to live at peace with whites in the area left to them. Certain strategic sites were reserved by the United States for posts and roads in the Indian country. In return, the United States gave the tribes $20,000 worth of goods immediately, and promised $9,500 more annually. Many Indians lingered in lands they had given up, and there were sporadic Indian outbreaks, especially during the War of 1812. However, the Greenville Treaty broke Indian resistance and made possible western expansion for the entire republic, which now numbered fifteen states.

Little Turtle, the Indiana-born Miami chief who so successfully led his race against Harmar and St. Clair, recognized a more powerful adversary in Wayne and counseled peace. Once on good terms with the English, he turned against them when they closed their stockade, Fort Miami, to the Indians seeking British protection after Fallen Timbers. His people, deserted by their British allies and vanquished by Wayne, must surrender their lands, he felt. For his support he was granted an annuity by the United States, and subsequently visited a number of American cities, where he was well received. But he lost caste with his tribe.

Wayne left behind him a string of forts from southern Ohio to the lake. These, no longer needed, fell gradually into ruin. Anthony Wayne Parkway Board is restoring many of them, along with later historic relics like canal locks and important early buildings. The Parkway, when finished, will touch twenty-three Ohio counties from Hamilton on the Ohio River to Lucas at Lake Erie.

HAMILTON COUNTY, 1790

Named for Alexander Hamilton

CINCINNATI still savours the compliments of Charles Dickens, so acidly critical of most places visited in his American tour of 1842. ". . . a beautiful city; cheerful, thriving, animated. I have not often seen a place that commends itself so favorably and pleasantly to a stranger at first glance. I was quite charmed with the town . . ." The city, as Dickens noted, had a "population of 50,000 souls." It was sixth in the United States, already the "Queen City of the West," a title acquired so early its origin is obscure. Cleveland in 1842 was only a bit over 6,000, a struggling pioneer town that ranked forty-fifth in the country.

By 1850 Cincinnati had soared to 116,000, despite recurring cholera which in 1849 took 4,000 lives. Cincinnati was the colorful gateway to all America, and her Ohio River trade was her lifeblood. Steamboats loaded passengers and freight, bound to and from the far south and inland Ohio; free Negroes singing chanteys shifted cargoes while their brothers moved southward in chains; gold-lured adventurers outfitted for the West; humble homesteaders rubbed elbows with elite tourists. A young Pennsylvanian, Stephen Foster, clerk in a riverside accounting house, took it all in and wrote some of his first songs, among them *O, Susanna*. After he left, he put his vivid impressions into such immortal folk tunes as *My Old Kentucky Home* and *Old Black Joe*. In Alms Park, Cincinnati placed a statue of Foster, looking out toward Kentucky hills. Harriet Beecher Stowe, brokenhearted over the loss of a little son from cholera, was packing to move east, where she would describe in *Uncle Tom's Cabin* the slavery picture which had unfolded here before her. The state maintains as a public memorial to Mrs. Stowe the home of her father Lyman Beecher, where she spent most of her eighteen years in Cincinnati. It is an odd historical coincidence that Foster and Mrs. Stowe, unacquainted with each other, were living in Cincinnati at the same time, both absorbing inspiration from the city.

The canal and two railroads brought prosperity. It rode, like some of the city's urchins, on the backs of hogs which loud-voiced drovers

Hamilton County. Looking across the Ohio River to the skyline of Cincinnati. The bridge was built in the 1860s.

herded through the main streets. The city was the world's greatest pork-packing center, and often was called Porkopolis. A tidal wave of Germans, fleeing the fatherland's militarism, swept in to join earlier settler groups of New Englanders and Kentuckians. Soon German was the language of many schools, churches and newspapers. The Rhinelanders brought their beer, their wine-growing and their music. Their concerts attracted patrons from surrounding Ohio and Kentucky communities. Music lovers organized the Cincinnati Symphony Orchestra, one of the early orchestras in the United States, and the far-famed May Music Festivals; the Conservatory of Music was established in 1867 by Clara Baur, German-trained musician; summer opera with casts from New York City's Metropolitan was presented in the Zoological Gardens.

In 1858 the University of Cincinnati, Ohio's first municipally-owned university, opened. Years before, Xavier, a Catholic university, was organized. The Ohio Mechanics Institute, where Thomas Edison was a student, was one of the first in the nation to teach the mechanical arts. Hebrew Union College, the first Jewish theological school in the United States, was supported by Cincinnati's learned and wealthy Jews, who always have had a leading part in the city's life. The first Jewish religious service in the Northwest Territory took place in the city in 1819.

The Civil War divided Cincinnati. Contacts with the South brought sympathy for the Confederate cause, and the *Enquirer* branded Lincoln a tyrant. It was also a union recruit center, and the headquarters for the Anti-Slavery Society and abolition newspapers.

The world's first professional baseball team, the Red Stockings, now the Cincinnati Reds, was launched in 1869, winning every game that year.

Pioneer Cincinnatians erected such impressive classic structures as St. Peter in Chains Cathedral, and the Taft Museum, built as a home in 1820 and later the residence of Charles P. Taft, whose brother, William Howard Taft, stood in 1908 at its pillared entrance to receive the nomination for the presidency of the United States. The Charles Tafts in 1928 gave the house to the city. Its art collection, established by the Art Museum in Eden Park and the Art Academy, added to Cincinnati's reputation as an art center. One of the oldest houses is The Pines, on Erie Street, home of former Governor and Mrs. Myers Y. Cooper, the latter, founder of the Martha Kinney Cooper Ohioana Library in Columbus. Its purpose is to promote the work of Ohio authors, and it is the only library of its kind in the country.

Today, a city so large that its suburbs spill over most of Hamilton County and into Kentucky as well, Cincinnati clings to tradition but is daringly progressive, too. It has an ultra-modern hotel eight stories above an office building, and one of the country's most up-to-date and beautiful railroad stations. Early Cincinnati led the west in culture with its Literary Club, the oldest such club west of the Alleghenies; with more books and periodicals published than anywhere else in the state. Today it leads the world in the manufacture of machine tools, playing cards, soap and electrotypes. The city is also within the orbit of the vast industrial development spreading through Ohio River communities since World War II.

The older businesses stem from pioneer times. William Procter and James Gamble married sisters and went into partnership to create the world's biggest soap factory. Other early soap makers, Werk and Jergens, were Germans like the Fleischmanns of yeast fame. Wurlitzer was a violin-playing piano manufacturer, and a German-speaking Swiss watchmaker named Gruen started still another industry. Rookwood Potteries, established in 1880 by Maria Longworth Storer, granddaughter of Nicholas Longworth, leading pioneer, is world-renowned. The pottery is on Mount Adams, site of the first Weather Bureau in the United States and of Ohio's first observatory.

One blot on the city's fair history is the reign of "Boss" George Cox, former tavern keeper, who, for more than twenty-five years, controlled votes, jobs and municipal politics. The scandalous epoch finally ended in 1924 with a city charter, and city management form of government. Cincinnati, for a time one of the worst governed, became one of the best governed communities.

Though explorers, traders and frontiersmen touched the spot years before, Cincinnati's birthdate is officially 1788. In 1802, Cincinnati, the county seat, was incorporated. Only forty years later Dickens was describing the city as one of the loveliest in America.

CLERMONT COUNTY, 1800

The name probably suggested by that of a French town

HIRAM ULYSSES was the name the Grants gave their son, born in 1822. They were living in a two-room cabin in the Ohio River village of Point Pleasant. The father, Jesse, had a hard time making a living and soon left for Georgetown. The baby grew into a freckled-faced, painfully shy boy, went about barefoot in tattered clothes, did hard farm work and never read a book if he could help it. Playmates nicknamed him "Hug" for the initials of his name. It was changed later through an error at West Point to Ulysses S. Grant.

The humble house, spruced up now with fresh paint, is a public museum. Grant was the country's Civil War hero, and in 1868 was elected eighteenth president of the United States with a rousing majority. He was the first native Ohio President, though Virginia-born William Henry Harrison, because of his long residence in the state, is generally listed as the first from Ohio. Following the collapse of a

199

Clermont County. The cottage at Point Pleasant in which Ulysses S. Grant was born in 1822. It is now a state memorial.

private investment venture, Grant at the end of his career was penniless. To support his family he wrote his memoirs, finishing them, despite severe and painful illness, only four days before his death. The work brought his family a half million dollars. He is buried in an imposing tomb on Riverside Drive, New York City.

Clermont County was the gateway for slaves fleeing across the Ohio River on the long journey to freedom in Canada. In the pillared mansion of Robert Fee at the little town of Moscow, a light was left burning as a beacon for the Negroes. The Fees, even their daughters, slept with loaded shotguns beside them as protection against the slave hunters. In Bethel lived Thomas Morris, a United States senator in the 1830s who opposed John C. Calhoun's and Henry Clay's proslavery utterances. He was one of the first officials to come out in the open against slavery, and his stand cost him his political career. ✓

River towns like Moscow, New Richmond, Neville and Chio were all but wiped off the map by the 1937 flood. Neville was named for a Revolutionary War officer from Virginia, who early in the 1800s took up over 1,000 acres here in military bounty lands.

200

At one of the first camp meetings in Ohio in 1816 the speaker was the eccentric pioneer evangelist Lorenzo Dow. Dow's pale face and piercing eyes were framed by a long beard and a thick mane of hair. Vast crowds assembled at the outdoor religious meetings when he was on the program. He rode from meeting to meeting on a small pony at a furious pace. He would dismount, lash his hearers for their sins, call on them to repent, then mount his horse, and tear through the woods to his next engagement. The camp meeting, which developed particularly in Kentucky and southern Ohio, was a unique institution of the frontier. It brought religion to settlers who had no other opportunity for church attendance, and it gave families living on lonely homesteads their only social contacts.

Batavia, the county seat, now a village of 1,500, had its first settler in 1797. He was a Virginia veteran, whose tiny cabin was the only habitation in the section for many years.

Utopia, a little village hugging the Ohio, was so named when a judge founded a communistic society here in 1844. This lasted only a few years, when Spiritualists took it over briefly until driven out by a severe flood.

BUTLER COUNTY, 1803

Named for General Richard Butler, killed in 1791 at St. Clair's defeat

A SHY, bespectacled young man rode his horse slowly into the beautiful town of Oxford to teach languages and philosophy at the recently opened Miami University. He was William Holmes McGuffey, twenty-five. The next year, 1826, he started work on a series of graded readers. During the ten years he spent at Miami he brought out four. Before his death, in 1873, and for a quarter-century longer, McGuffey's Eclectic Readers were the accepted textbooks of the schools of America. An estimated 140,000,000 copies were sold. They brought their author less than $1,000 in royalties, but they shaped the minds of the country culturally and morally.

Butler County. William Holmes McGuffey began work on his famous school readers while a professor at Miami University, Oxford.

A well-versed scholar, McGuffey culled the world's best literature for excerpts for his volumes. With pedagogical genius, with short sentences for beginners and appealing illustrations, he suited his lessons to children's years. While learning to read boys and girls shared in the world's rich storehouse of knowledge. In countless homes, these books were the only reading matter, pored over by the children and by their elders as well. Up to McGuffey's time, little attention was given to books for children, who were reared on stilted primers and works like *Pilgrim's Progress* and Foxe's *Book of Martyrs*. McGuffey, a product of the frontier himself, preached what the pioneer understood: rugged individualism; the virtue of hard work; the sure reward of goodness. At Miami University there is a McGuffey monument and museum, where the growing cult of McGuffey enthusiasts meet each June to honor him.

Miami University, one of six state-supported colleges, is second oldest in the state. The legislature set aside a township to finance the institution.

At Oxford, Western College for Women was chartered in 1853. It was a pioneer college exclusively for women in which they might enjoy the same educational opportunities as those provided in men's colleges.

Hamilton is the county seat, a broad-streeted city of 60,000 which combines teeming commerce with fine old homes and aristocratic traditions. The city makes a big percentage of the country's vaults and bank safes and many paper products, and has one of the largest stove factories in the world. Ludlow Park, named for the town's founder, contains a monument topped by a hollow globe. It is a memorial to Captain John Cleves Symmes, namesake of his pioneer landowner uncle. The captain believed that the world was hollow and habitable on the interior, with a passage at the North Pole to this "rich, warm land."

Another Miami Valley industrial city, Middletown, started its present paper mills in pioneer times. Tobacco, raised in surrounding valley farms, brought new industry and a large factory and added to the city's commerce. In 1900 George M. Verity built the American Rolling Mills Company, Armco, which now has plants and offices around the world; he pioneered in setting up one of the first laboratories for steel research in 1910; in developing the continuous rolling mill process which changed steel-making and, in the World War I period, inaugurating forward-looking worker-management policies. The chairman of the board, Charles R. Hook, came to Armco during its first decade.

James A. Campbell of Hamilton, Ohio governor·in 1890, a manufacturer of ballot boxes, introduced the secret ballot, whereby voters could mark their tickets and drop them in a box. Before that they had to tell election clerks how they wanted to vote. Murat Halstead (1829–1908), editor of the *Cincinnati Commercial*, a prolific writer who influenced Ohio political trends, was born in Butler County. Kenesaw Mountain Landis (1866–1944), the Chicago judge who became "czar" of the major baseball leagues in 1920, was a native of Millville.

WARREN COUNTY, 1803

Named for General Joseph Warren, killed in the Battle of Bunker Hill

THREE solemn-faced strangers in broad-brimmed hats and oddly cut black suits knocked at the door of a pious farmer in Lebanon one cold morning in March 1805. They had walked, they said, 1,000 miles from New Lebanon, New York, guided by a heavenly host and sent out by Mother Ann, an Englishwoman leader of the United Society of Believers in the Second Appearing of Christ. Sometimes they were called Shakers, the men added. The message of these missionaries, the first Shakers to come west, fell on responsive hearts, for it was a period of great religious unrest. By May a dozen families had deeded their farms to be held in common by the society. Husbands and wives renounced family relations to live as brothers and sisters, consecrated to the Lord. In a few years Union Village, on the edge of Lebanon, controlled 4,500 acres in the fertile valley of Turtle Creek, named for Chief Little Turtle. The wealthy vigorous community was self-sustaining, numbered 600 Believers and had 150 sturdy buildings. Work was part of the Shakers' religion. The Poland China hog, introduced by them, became so important that Warren County put up an eight-foot marble statue near Lebanon to this breed of swine.

Like all nineteenth-century communal experiments, the Shaker movement lost favor with the young. Celibacy further diminished numbers. In 1913 the remaining handful of Shakers sold their holdings. Union Village, with its old Shaker buildings, is now operated by the Evangelical-United Brethren Church as a center for orphans and the aged, called Otterbein Home. The name is in honor of the United Brethren Church founder. The Shaker story still lives in the fine old buildings like the residence of the "Center Family," now one of the homes for children. Its two stairways, one for men, the other for women, lead to the one-time women's and men's separate quarters. A big second floor room retains the uncomfortable wall benches where Shakers rested when not in the center of the floor going through their intricate religious dances and marches.

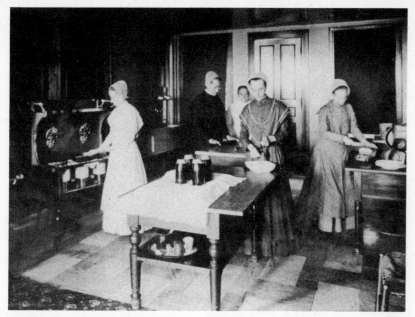

Warren County. Shaker kitchen at Union Village, near Lebanon, the first and largest Ohio settlement of this religious sect.

While the thrifty Shakers were developing their village, Lebanon was building the distinguished homes which give it its architectural fame. In 1836 skilled journeymen fashioned a fine Greek Revival home, called Glendower. Little changed through the years, it was purchased by local subscription in 1945 and is now the Warren County Museum. Each spring county and town unite in arranging pilgrimages to homes built during Lebanon's Golden Age. In Lebanon, not far from Glendower, is Ohio's oldest hotel, the Golden Lamb. A license to operate "a house of publick entertainment" was issued to the first building on this site in 1803. The present structure dates from 1815 and is furnished throughout in the vogue of the last century.

In a county claiming many illustrious sons, the most notable was Thomas Corwin (1794–1865), Ohio's greatest orator. He was elected to the Ohio legislature, to the governorship of Ohio, to the United States House and Senate; he was also appointed President Fillmore's Secretary of the Treasury and ambassador to Mexico by Lincoln.

One of Ohio's oldest weekly newspapers, the *Western Star*, has been printed in Lebanon continuously since its founding in 1807.

Near Lebanon is Fort Ancient, a series of forts and village sites. Earthen walls extend over three miles along a hill overlooking the Little Miami River and enclose 100 acres. The remains are in a state-owned park of 700 acres, where a museum exhibits artifacts made by the vanished people who were advanced craftsmen. Among the quaint little villages so numerous in Warren County one of the oldest is Waynesville, founded by English settlers in 1796 and named for Anthony Wayne.

PREBLE COUNTY, 1808

Named for Captain Edward Preble, naval commander

THE WEEK before Christmas, 1864, a sad young man chalked a song on the blackboard of his singing school at New Paris. Benjamin Hanby was thirty-one, though his heavy thatch of black beard made him appear older. The song was his own composition. He was surprised, and cheered a little, as the children went through the verses with dancing eyes, and burst joyously into the lilting chorus:

> O, O, O, who wouldn't go!
> O, O, O, who wouldn't go!
> Up on the housetop, click, click, click!
> Down through the chimney with Good St. Nick!

The jolly simple carol which he called *Santa Claus* had the touch of genius on it, and since that day has been sung by millions of children in many lands and languages. But until recently, Hanby received no credit for it. He died three years after he wrote it, and never learned of its triumphal popularity. He did know that another of his songs, *Darling Nellie Gray*, was being sung at every Union campfire. It was based on the pathetic love story of a fugitive slave who had died at the Hanby home in Rushville while on the way to Canada to purchase freedom for his Georgia sweetheart, Nellie Gray. The Hanbys later

Preble County. Fort St. Clair Park at Eaton.

moved to Westerville, where young Hanby prepared for the ministry in the United Brethren Church.

Hanby's first pastorate was at Lewisburg, Preble County. When he introduced a little foot-pumped organ to accompany the hymn singing, parishioners objected. Music in a church was sacrilegious, they thought. Hanby moved on to a charge in New Paris in the same county, near the Indiana border, taking his organ with him. The issue reasserted itself, and he resigned in anguish of soul. He was a devout man who had dedicated his life to the church. But he was also a musician, and felt music was part of God's ministry. He rented an empty storeroom in New Paris and opened a singing school, where he preached as well as taught music.

Some of his best songs were written during his stay in Preble County. News of his activities reached George F. Root, Chicago musical publisher, who had composed such successes as *Tramp, Tramp, Tramp, the Boys are Marching* and *Just Before the Battle, Mother.* He asked Hanby to collaborate with him at a salary that seemed princely to the hard-pressed Hanby. Hanby's *Santa Claus* melody was first published by this firm in 1866, with only Hanby's initials signed to it. Shortly after, he became too ill to attend to his affairs, and the music house, swept by the great Chicago fire, went out of business. Hanby's identity with the Christmas song was lost. Through recent research by Ohioans, it was discovered that in his short, troubled life he wrote eighty songs, hymns and minstrel airs.

Near Eaton, the county seat, a town of 4,300, is Fort St. Clair State Park. Under a famed whispering oak are the graves of men killed in an Indian attack on the fort. In Eaton's old Mound cemetery is buried "Father" James Finley, Methodist circuit rider. He spent his life on horseback winning converts from Lake Erie to the Ohio River. His most successful mission was among the Wyandots in Upper Sandusky. Finley and his bride started married life in a southern Ohio forest cabin. "No couple on earth lived happier," says Finley in his exciting frontier autobiography.

MONTGOMERY COUNTY, 1803

Named for General Richard Montgomery, killed at Montreal in 1775

ON A back page of the *Dayton Journal*, December 19, 1903, appeared a few lines about the "Clever Device of Bishop Wright's Sons." They had telegraphed their father from Kitty Hawk, North Carolina, that they had completed "four successful flights" two days before "against a twenty-one-mile wind," and made "an average speed of thirty-one miles, staying in the air 57 seconds." The brief news item meant that Dayton henceforth would be heralded as the birthplace of aviation.

The Wrights' fragile boxlike plane, the first engine-powered airplane, was put together in a bicycle shop on a Dayton side street where for years Wilbur, then thirty-six, and his brother Orville, thirty-two, had been tinkering with kites and wind currents. Today Dayton's Wright-Patterson Air Force Base is the research and procurement center of the United States Air Force, with 1,780 acres and over 1,000 buildings. In the fifty years since the Kitty Hawk flight has come the sabre jet plane, weighing over 13,000 pounds and flying

670 mph. From Dayton in 1910 the first air freight, a bolt of cloth, was carried and delivered to a Columbus department store.

More than twenty years before, another Dayton invention, the Incorruptible Cashier, a "mechanical money drawer," rang its bell for the first time in the restaurant of James Ritty, who patented the machine. A few years later, a local manufacturer, John H. Patterson, bought the rights for $6,500, immediately regretting his purchase. Stuck with it, he went to work to improve the contraption. From his efforts emerged the National Cash Register Company. The cash register changed the retail storekeeping habits of the world, and made Dayton one of the great industrial centers of the country.

Shortly after the Wrights' achievement, Charles F. Kettering fashioned an electric starting motor for the cash register. He experimented further, and in 1910 came up with that great boon to motorists, the self-starter, which boomed automobile manufacture. Kettering's genius pushed him into many lines, including a company for making farm electric light systems which was later absorbed by General Motors. This corporation established giant plants in Dayton, including those for the manufacture of electric refrigerators. The city also forged ahead in the making of precision tools.

By 1950 Dayton had a population of 250,000. The city developed with style. Built at the confluence of four rivers, the Miami, Mad, Stillwater and Wolf Creek, it looped itself gracefully around the streams. It laid out extra wide thoroughfares, built graceful bridges over its rivers, and placed its handsome buildings well out of the path of factory smoke.

The only checks were recurring floods. In 1913, the four rivers went on a rampage in the worst flood of all. Waters rose throughout the whole Miami Valley, taking more than 350 lives and destroying $100,000,000 worth of property. The disaster pushed Dayton into organizing the Miami Conservancy District, under able Arthur E. Morgan. The flood threat was ended forever in the valley with a $32 million water control system, the first of its kind in the world. Dayton shook off the muddy residue of the flood, built new and bigger plants, finer buildings, parks, an art institute, a carillon. The fine old classic courthouse of Dayton limestone withstood the engulfing waters as did Dayton's first dwelling, George Newcomb's two-story log cabin.

Montgomery County. Air view of Dayton, showing the Great Miami River.

It was built shortly after four Revolutionary War veterans, headed by General Arthur St. Clair, purchased 60,000 acres here from John Cleves Symmes. Among the surveyors was Jonathan Dayton, whose name was given to the settlement that began in 1796, as soon as Wayne's peace treaty made the area safe from Indian attack.

National attention was turned on Dayton in 1863 when street rioting broke out in sympathy with a Dayton senator and newspaper editor, Clement L. Vallandigham. A "Copperhead" or "Peace Democrat," he was arrested for his anti-Union utterances. Vallandigham was tried and convicted of treason and banished by Lincoln to Confederate lines. He went to Bermuda, and from there to Canada where he learned the Ohio Democrats had nominated him for governor. However, he lost the election to John Brough. Following the war, Vallandigham returned to law practice in Ohio, dying in the Golden Lamb Hotel in Lebanon after accidentally shooting himself. He is buried in Dayton's Woodland Cemetery, the resting place also of the poet Paul Laurence Dunbar, Negro native of the city who died at thirty-four. While the Wright brothers were flying their early planes, Dunbar was going up and down as elevator operator in a Dayton business block, dreaming about his graceful lyrics in Negro dialect. His Dayton home, now a state museum, bears the inscription from his pen:

> Because I had loved so deeply,
> Because I had loved so long,
> God in his great compassion
> Gave me the gift of song.

Zoos in many parts of the world benefited from Sol Stephan's scientific knowledge about wild animals. He was born in Dayton in 1849 and for years was in charge of the zoo at Cincinnati. His son and grandson followed him in the work. A prominent Daytonian is James M. Cox, native of Butler County, three times governor of Ohio, defeated in 1920 by another Ohioan, Harding, for president of the United States. Cox, wealthy owner of several newspapers, maintains an estate which is one of the show spots in Dayton.

GREENE COUNTY, 1803

Named for General Nathaniel Greene, second in command under Washington during the Revolutionary War

ALL OF Greene County, it seemed, came to Yellow Springs that crisp day in October 1853, for the opening of Antioch College and the inauguration of its president, the great Horace Mann. The new college was non-sectarian, with the twin aims of high scholarship and equal opportunities for women and men, including Negroes. No better choice for president could have been made than Mann, hailed for his Massachusetts public school reforms and his spicy antislavery debates with Daniel Webster when both were United States congressmen. Yellow Spring citizens had pledged $30,000 and a 20-acre campus. Mann, with his wife Mary, a sister of Mrs. Nathaniel Hawthorne, and their three little boys, made the

Greene County. The twin towers of Old Antioch, Antioch College, Yellow Springs.

difficult 1,000-mile journey from Boston. In the family portfolio was a picture of two Gothic college buildings, a fine president's house set amidst a landscaped campus. They found one building far from finished, the president's house without a roof, and the campus a shambles. Mann, with the flashing eyes and snow-white hair, talked from an open air platform to the eager upturned faces of 3,000 who had come by wagon and shiny carriages for the inaugural.

Finances worried Mann from the start. Pledges were not forthcoming, faculty members, tiring of teaching without salaries, resigned. Mann, refusing many lucrative offers elsewhere, dipped freely into personal funds and stayed on. The staggering odds were too much. He died in 1859, worn out at fifty-three. One crisis followed another and the college steadily declined.

In 1920 Antioch righted itself and its present successful era began under President Arthur E. Morgan, who had engineered the Miami Flood Control project and was to become head of the Tennessee Valley Authority. Horace Mann's philosophy still hovers over his college. His motto, "Be afraid to die until you have won some victory for humanity," is carved on his statue prominently placed in the 1,000-acre Glen Helen woodland, added to the campus by the gift of an alumnus, Hugh Birch, one-time playmate of Mann's boys.

To the south a few miles, near Xenia, the county seat, another forward-looking educational effort, Wilberforce University, was launched. Stemming from a seminary in a Columbus church basement for the schooling of Negro youth, Tawawa Springs health resort was remodeled in 1856 as a university named for the English abolitionist, William Wilberforce. Closed during the Civil War, it was reopened by the African Methodist Episcopal Church. It was one of the country's first permanent institutions for the education of Negroes. An early president was the self-taught Bishop Daniel Payne, a former slave. The University's Payne Theological Seminary is named for him. The college, like all pioneer schools, was harassed by lack of funds, and by fires. In a reorganization in 1951, two institutions emerged: Wilberforce University, supported by the African Methodist Episcopal Church, and Central State College, financed by state appropriations. The two use practically the same wooded campus, with only a bridged ravine between them.

Born near Cedarville was Whitelaw Reid, publisher of the New York *Tribune*, minister to France and ambassador to England. A Xenia resident, Coates Kinney (1826–1904), was known far and wide for his poem, "Rain on the Roof."

A little village to the north of Xenia with the odd name of Oldtown is actually one of the oldest in Ohio. It was an already venerable Indian settlement when visited in 1778 by Daniel Boone.

CLARK COUNTY, 1817

Named for George Rogers Clark

TWENTY-EIGHT-YEAR-OLD   George Rogers Clark tossed his coonskin cap high in the air, brushed the long black hair from his eyes and called on fellow-Kentuckians for revenge.

213

Clark County. The Madonna of the Trail, near Springfield, was erected in memory of the pioneer wives and mothers who journeyed westward over the National Road (Route 40).

Shawnees, he said, had massacred a group of Kentucky traders as the men were mooring their boats on the Ohio. In retaliation, he proposed a foray into the Shawnees' homeland in the Ohio Country. The previous year, 1779, Clark had won the vast Northwest from the British in what was the western phase of the Revolutionary War. Those exploits made him the hero of the frontier, and its leader. He had no trouble collecting a band for the expedition he proposed into the Ohio wilderness. Almost before he finished speaking the men around him started oiling muskets and filling powder horns. Daniel Boone and Simon Kenton jumped at the chance to go along.

Crossing the Ohio River, they cached supplies at the mouth of the Miami and moved cautiously north into the valley of the Mad River to a place near today's Springfield. The Indians checked Clark's band at first. Then he let go a volley or two from a cannon he somehow had managed to drag along, and the Shawnees fled in terror. Watching the whole engagement from the crotch of a tall tree was a twelve-year-old Indian lad, Tecumseh. When he climbed down to join his defeated tribesmen, he vowed he would dedicate his life to fighting white men. Later, as a powerful Shawnee chief, he made good his pledge. However, he never countenanced brutality, and for his humane policies he was much respected by settlers even though they knew he was their foe. After Clark's defeat of the Shawnees, Indian attacks lessened and the area became safe for settlement. Springfield's official founding date, however, is 1801, when a wandering surveyor laid out the town. Before the ink was dry on the plat, Griffith Foos arrived and opened a tavern. Under its hospitable roof, Springfield was born, and today the inn site at Main and Spring Streets is marked with a plaque. After the Shawnee raid, Kenton came a second time, this time to stake a claim beside Buck Creek. Many Kentuckians followed to settle near their hero. By the time the county was organized Springfield was big enough to be chosen as the seat of government.

The town came alive in the 1830s when the National Road reached it, doing for Springfield what canals accomplished for other inland Ohio settlements. On the pike near Springfield is a statue, the Madonna of the Trail, erected by the Daughters of the American Revolution in memory of pioneer wives and mothers who endured the joltings of the road in early times.

The mid-1800s saw the start of farm machinery manufacture, destined to become a leading local industry. William Whiteley invented a binder and organized a plant that expanded into the biggest of its kind in the world. Subsequently it was absorbed by the International Harvester Company. During the early era of farm implement manufacture, P. P. Mast put out a modest house organ, *Farm and Fireside*. He intended it only as an advertisement for the cultivator he was developing, but the publication grew into one of the country's important agricultural magazines. It was the basis for Springfield's plant of the Crowell-Collier Publishing Company, which today prints millions of copies of several national magazines. By 1950 Springfield's population was almost 80,000.

The 4-H Club movement, which has spread to every civilized country and enriched the lives of 12,000,000 boys and girls, was started in a basement room in the Springfield courthouse. In the 1890s a country schoolteacher, A. B. Graham, took what he called his Agricultural Clubs there on Saturday afternoons because the school board disapproved of his talks on better farm techniques and home management being presented in his classroom. Word of his clubs reached Ohio State University which invited Graham to become supervisor of agricultural extension clubs for boys and girls, the first such job in the country. He organized on a national basis these boys' and girls' clubs, which eventually adopted the name 4-H Clubs, the H standing for head, heart, hand and health, with a four-leaf-clover design as emblem.

Overlooking Springfield is the landscaped campus of Wittenberg College founded by the Lutherans in 1845. The George Rogers Clark Memorial State Park on the city's outskirts honors the daring frontiersman who had so much to do with starting settlement in the county that is named for him.

DARKE COUNTY, 1816

Named for General William Darke, who served under General Arthur St. Clair at his defeat in 1791

"THE ground where this council house stands is unstained with blood . . . I wish nothing so much as peace and brotherly love . . . while we await your brothers we will have refreshment. and drink to wash the dust from our throats . . . and to make merry, but not passing the bounds of sobriety."

So spoke General Anthony Wayne. Soldier, now turned diplomat, he was host to 1,100 Indians at Fort Greenville in the summer of 1795. Among those who were present were Tahre, the Crane, chief of the federated Wyandots, Leatherlips, White Pigeon, Bad Bird, Black Hoof and Buckongehelas. Belligerent Blue Jacket had to be bribed with a three-hundred-dollar gift. Tecumseh did not come. The chiefs with retainers, their women and children, dogs and horses, began straggling in as early as June for treaty talks which were not concluded until August. As the first of the warriors arrived, soldiers were hoisting in place the final logs for the formidable stockade which enclosed 50 acres in what is the heart of today's Greenville. Inside were log huts for the soldiers and a huge council house where the deliberations were held. It was Wayne's difficult task to keep the Indians contented during the long negotiations, to furnish them with food sumptuous enough to impress them, and with enough liquor to satisfy them without making them unruly. His own troops, about 2,400, had to be provided for also. In the remote wilderness it was a colossal undertaking.

He had sent runners with 100 invitations written by his young aide de camp, William Henry Harrison, to chiefs throughout Ohio. He familiarized himself with the curious and labored Indian peace ritual, aided by his interpreters, Isaac Zane and William Wells. Both had Indian wives and were trusted by the tribes.

Wayne, firm, blunt and cajoling, finally molded them into agreement and got their marks on the parchment. The Indians were to keep the peace and hunt west and north of a line running south and west from Cleveland to today's Mercer County, and south along the

Darke County. Annie Oakley, greatest woman sharpshooter.

Ohio boundary line to the Ohio River. A detachment of Wayne's dragoons rushed the precious treaty to Philadelphia where George Washington signed it. It is now in the National Archives at Washington, D.C. A copy was given to Tahre. Wayne kept the peace pipe which had been used, and it is now in the Ohio State Museum at Columbus.

Every August Greenville Boy Scouts rekindle Wayne's peace fire in the beautiful Fort Greenville Treaty Memorial Park. Wayne's stockade has been reproduced in miniature. Greenville, the county seat, a city of 9,000, has a number of thriving industries but is proudest of its Indian peace tradition.

Darke County's most illustrious daughter, born Annie Moses, was better known as Annie Oakley. When Annie was ten she took down her dead father's muzzleloader, heavier than she thought, loaded it, and carried it out to the woods near the cabin. In a few minutes she had a nice fat rabbit. She knew it was the only food except some ground corn, which the family would have for supper that night. After that she went out every day with the gun, bagging rabbits, pheasant and quail, shooting the birds through their heads to save the meat. Tavern keepers in nearby Greenville, Cincinnati and Dayton were glad to have her game. When she was fourteen she entered a Cincinnati match with a celebrated shot, Frank Butler. Annie wore a pink cotton dress she had made, a floppy sunbonnet and her hair in braids. As the awkward backwoods girl aimed her clumsy gun, Butler and the audience smiled. But not for long. Annie won the meet and the fifty-dollar prize. The event started her on the career which was to make her the world's best woman marksman. At nineteen she married Butler. The two were never separated though she soon outshone him. She was the star attraction as "Little Sure Shot" in Buffalo Bill's Wild West show, the Forpaugh-Sells and P. T. Barnum circuses. Annie performed amazing tricks. Her most celebrated feat, perforating cards tossed in the air, gives us the phrase "Annie Oakleys," meaning complimentary theater tickets—they are punched with holes like those Annie put in the cards.

Annie Oakley died in 1926, at the age of sixty-six. Her ashes, placed in a silver cup won at one of her matches, are buried beside her husband's in a little cemetery near Brock in northern Darke County.

MIAMI COUNTY, 1807

Named for the Miami Indians, the first inhabitants of the Miami Valley

RACHEL, a Philadelphia Quaker miss, very pretty in her dove-gray dress and white fichu, was sixteen, and too young, her father thought, for marriage. Anyway the strapping Irishman, John Johnston, with the twinkling eyes and the firm chin, was not a Friend. Rachel could not marry outside of Meeting. So, one night when the clouds pulled darkness over the moon, Rachel tiptoed out the back door, and was swung up on a fast horse behind her lover. The two galloped off to a minister, and then on, 1,000 miles into the Ohio wilderness near the Indian village called Piqua. Johnston had been appointed Indian factor that year, 1809, by his friend, President James Madison. Indians still lingered in the Ohio northwest despite the Greenville Treaty. Though peace had settled for a time,

Miami County. The three-story red brick colonial home, built near Piqua in 1814 by Colonel John Johnson, Indian agent.

trouble was stirring from British proddings—a prelude to the war that was to come in 1812.

Two years after his arrival, Johnston built his twenty-roomed frontier mansion, today one of the few Indian agency houses extant in America. Outside doors were double, with hand-forged iron bolts against possible attack. A narrow stairway wound to the roof where aides kept constant vigil for marauding tribes.

Johnston was sincerely interested in the Indians and his kindliness and helpfulness soon won them. He had arrived in America from Ireland at the age of seventeen, in time to drive a supply wagon in Pennsylvania for Anthony Wayne and later, promoted to colonel, to accompany him to the Greenville Treaty meeting. When Charles Dickens made his American tour, Johnston was one of the Americans he especially wanted to see.

Rachel lived long as the lady of the manor, becoming the mother of fifteen children. She founded one of America's first women's clubs, Piqua's Female Bible Society.

The city of Piqua, now grown to 18,000, is nestled engagingly in a bend of the Great Miami. Long before white settlers filtered in, Indians had villages here, always called Piqua. The name came from a Shawnee legend. As a great campfire faded out, its embers were stirred and a man stepped forth—piqua, man born of ashes. Indian settlements here were ravaged repeatedly by militia clearing the land as if it belonged to whites. The Shawnees returned again and again to mourn beside the graves of their fallen, hoping piqua would come true and they could bring life back from the ashes.

The first white settlers called the town Washington, but in 1816 gave it its earlier Indian name, Piqua. Church spires cut up through the trees. Bridges span the winding river. Houses within the city proper, like those of the landed gentry on the surrounding farms, are among the best of Ohio's early architecture.

Troy, the county seat, is a city of 11,000. It is on the Miami, where in early days sand bars and rooted trees made voyaging a hazard. When the new courthouse was built it cost nearly half a million dollars, and was the most elaborate in the state. Troy's broad streets and its stately old houses, many of them brick, give the city a New England look. At one time it was famous for its buggy and wagon shops; today it is known for factories making kitchen equipment.

MERCER COUNTY, 1824

Named for General Hugh Mercer, who fell at the Battle of Princeton, 1777

WINTER was already in the air on November 3, 1791, when General Arthur St. Clair halted his grumbling army on the banks of the Wabash. It had been a hard march over rough trails from the comfortable Fort Jefferson which the men had built 30 miles to the south. They had been on the way since May, putting up stockades, marching, camping in the wilderness. Uniforms were worn and thin, and the expected warmer clothing had not come, nor the food rations, either. Much of the powder which had caught up with them would not ignite in their cannons. Nearly every night men crept off into the woods, until soon a total of 300 had deserted.

Except for some officers and a few companies of militia, the army was composed of adventurers picked up along the march. They were tired now of the whole affair. St. Clair, fifty-seven, was so crippled with gout and rheumatism that he had to be lifted on and off his horse. When President Washington ordered him to march against the Indians ravaging the western Ohio Country, the general was promised a trained army, adequate munitions and equipment. St. Clair was temperamentally unfit for Indian warfare, but he mapped a sound campaign. He decided to march to the confluence of the St. Mary and St. Joseph Rivers in the Indiana Territory, where Fort Wayne stands today. There he would awe and curb the "savages." Behind him he left a string of forts as supply and communication points.

St. Clair thought the river where he rested his exhausted men was the St. Mary. Actually he was seventy miles or so away. He dispatched to the rear a regiment he could little spare, to search for the long-overdue supply wagons and the deserters. The weary men of the main detachment threw themselves down on leaves and boughs for a night's rest.

St. Clair had planned to build a shelter and stockade here the next day, as his operations point. But before sunrise, as the soldiers were beginning to stir, the Indians, led by Little Turtle and Blue Jacket, attacked. There were hordes of them, no one knows how many. They surrounded the surprised troops who had no time to organize. There was valiant resistance for a time, but soon those still alive dashed off in disorderly retreat, throwing away their rifles, not stopping until they gained the security of Fort Jefferson. It was all over in a couple of hours. Dead and dying, 900 men and officers lay amidst a shambles of still and writhing horses, overturned artillery, guns and abandoned wagons. The Indians had bayonetted and tortured the wounded. Freshly scalped heads lay like bloody pumpkins in a frozen field. Three western Ohio counties, Butler, Clark and Darke, are named in memory of participating officers, killed or wounded. Washington, when the news reached him, broke into a fury of denunciation of his old friend, St. Clair. The general remained in Ohio, as governor of the Northwest Territory, but his star had set. The Indians, raised to new confidence, increased their depredations. Three years later, General Anthony Wayne quelled them, calling the spot Fort Recovery.

Mercer County. Fort Recovery, the site of St. Clair's defeat in 1791.

The Wabash was dammed in 1837 to make Grand Reservoir for the Miami-Erie Canal, now St. Mary's Lake. Construction took eight years and 1,700 men, working from sunrise to sunset. They were paid thirty cents a day and a jigger of whisky. The lake, a state-owned public recreation area since 1915, covers about 18,000 acres and has 52 miles of shoreline. When built it was the largest man-made body of water in the world.

Celina, the county seat, a town of 5,800, grew up around lumber mills and today has the world's biggest table factory, which daily turns out 2,000 of these furniture items.

In the western part of the county, settled by Germans, large Catholic churches dominate little villages named for the churches; St. John, St. Henry and St. Wendelin. One village, Maria Stein, takes its name from a convent founded in 1846. Many of the nuns are paid by public funds to teach in public schools of surrounding villages where practically all the children are Catholics. The convent has rare relics, such as portions of the True Cross and pieces of the girdle and veil of the Blessed Virgin.

SHELBY COUNTY, 1819

Named for General Isaac Shelby, a Revolutionary War officer and Kentucky governor

SHREWD Charles Starrett held title to extensive holdings along the Great Miami, where he put up a one-room shelter and farmed the grasslands. In 1820 he heard to his dismay that circuit judges were holding court in a pioneer cabin six miles away in a new settlement, Hardin. They were going to make it the seat of the new county, which was to be named Shelby. Starrett hunted up the commissioners. "I'll give you fifty acres, free, if you'll set up the county seat on my land." It was a sizable parcel and the deal went through.

The new town had to have a name. The commissioners rode over the narrow forest trail one bright spring day and reined their horses at Starrett's door. A sweep of open land dotted with wild flowers spread before them; beyond, the majestic Miami rippled in the sunshine. It reminded one among them of Sir Philip Sidney's "Arcadia," about a country of "flowery meadows so fair the people never grow old."

"I'd say call it Arcadia, except I hear there's a town named that already."

"Well, then, what about Sidney for its name?" his companion countered.

So, in the young state of Ohio, Sidney was born of a Yankee bargain and named for a sixteenth-century British poet. The new county seat, 65 miles west of Columbus, grew slowly, developing from a farm trading center into a busy manufacturing community. Its citizens are aware of the lurking romance of its setting in the old Miami River Valley. Diligently they erect markers and monuments and highway

Shelby County. The locks at Lockington on the Miami-Erie Canal. Now preserved as an historical site on the Anthony Wayne Parkway.

signs about gusty adventure of two hundred years ago when George Washington's emissary, the devout Christopher Gist, visited it. At that time it was the important Indian village, Pickawalliny, the home of the Miami tribe and the leather-faced tricky chief, Old Britain. His town was wiped out later by a posse of hot-headed Canadians who galloped into the beautiful valley, buckskin jackets flying and rifles cocked. Nearby was the trading post of a Frenchman, Peter Loramie, whose name remains on a local stream and on a large lake to the northwest, now a popular recreation spot.

Travelers coming from the south are struck by the spectacular bridge spanning the valley on five massively graceful arches. Above the city's clustered housetops rise church spires, among them those of the First Presbyterian and the Catholic Holy Angels. And in the heart of Sidney, on Starrett's one-time farm, is the ornate courthouse, a kind of memorial to his sagacity.

The Monumental Building on the square was built to honor Civil War heroes and financed through a town lottery. About the time the

225

building was going up, General James O. Amos, adjutant general of Ohio and founder of the Ohio National Guard, arrived in Sidney and bought the *Shelby Democrat*. In his paper's masthead he proclaimed it was "published for the benefit of the people and the pocketbook of the proprietor." From it emerged Sidney's present *Daily News*, in which members of the Amos family still are at the helm.

Lockington, originally Lockport, is a tiny village south of Sidney. It was created by the coming of the Miami-Erie canal and put to sleep by its going. The waterway left behind six magnificent hand-dressed stone locks, steps really, by which the water floated its burden of barges up the 67-foot rise of the Loramie Summit. It was the highest point in the canal between Cincinnati and Toledo, 500 feet above the Ohio River level. Another marvel of pioneer technique here is the stone aqueduct over which the canal, high in the air, crossed Loramie Creek. The surrounding lands now are part of the Anthony Wayne Parkway.

The little town of Russia—pronounced locally "Rooshie"—in western Shelby County was so named by French settlers who had marched under Napoleon into the land of the Cossacks. The endless plains and the first Ohio winter when the snowfall was heavy reminded the pioneers of Russia.

AUGLAIZE COUNTY, 1848

Named for the Auglaize River

GERMANS settled western Auglaize County a century or more ago, and the Old-World flavor persists. Minster, originally Muenster, is spic and span, with streets as neat as table tops and square brick houses close to the sidewalks. The big industry is a brewery, following the same formula as the first brew-masters brought with them from Cologne and Bavaria. Beer, aged in hillside caves in the early days, was peddled from kegs carted from house to house by horse-drawn wagons. Hops, malt and barley, once locally grown, now are imported. Minster was settled by Catholics, and their vaulted St. Augustine church is reminiscent of German

Auglaize County. The feeder and canal for Grand Lake, also called St. Marys Lake, near St. Marys.

cathedrals. The churches of New Bremen, its twin village, all are Protestant, and its industries are given mainly to woolen and blanket mills.

Blanket-making is also one of the industries at St. Marys, a town of 7,000. The town, gateway to beautiful St. Marys, on Grand Lake, is a resort and supply center for sportsmen. In frontier times when it was a busy Indian trading post, it was known as Girtys' Town, home of the evil brothers James, George, Thomas and Simon Girty, who roamed Ohio and joined forces with the British, and never missed a chance to harm their fellow-Americans.

East of St. Marys is Wapakoneta, the county seat, laid out in 1832 after the Shawnees moved beyond the Mississippi. Its early German settlers were clever woodworkers, and the town became nationally known for its toy and furniture plants. Shawnee and other tribes had settled here when they were driven from the area around Piqua by

227

George Rogers Clark. For decades the Indians in this area lived at peace with the white settlers, and adopted many civilized customs. This was due to the presence of an earnest band of Quaker missionaries under the devout and gentle Friend, Isaac Harvey. He taught them to farm and to use the horse instead of their women for carrying burdens. A woman's life was once spared by the Indians, "because Friend Harvey asked it." Harvey receives little attention from Ohio historians. Yet he probably did more to keep bloodshed from early Ohio than all the armies of Harmar, St. Clair and Wayne.

Jim Tully left an Auglaize County orphanage, where he was reared, to make his fortune as farm laborer, tree surgeon, circus roustabout and pugilist. He wove his experiences into novels which were best sellers in the 1920s. One book was dramatized by Maxwell Anderson as *Outside Looking In*. Tully became one of the highest paid promotion men in Hollywood.

VAN WERT COUNTY, 1837

Named for Isaac Van Wert (original spelling Van Wart), one of the captors of Major John André

A CLUMP of peonies planted in a backyard garden in Van Wert fifty years ago made the city the peony center of the Middle West. Neighbors caught the fever until every little home plot and all the tree lawns along principal streets bloomed in early summer with the heavy-headed flowers. Growers planted acres of them and went to France and England to secure rare types. The city's peony festival, with elaborate flower floats, became a national event, and Van Wert peonies won medals at the country's flower shows. Van Wert, the county seat, has grown to a city of 10,500 since it was founded in the 1830s.

Van Wert always has looked to its future. From 1850 on, its thrifty citizens began leaving substantial bequests to local welfare and cultural enterprises. Many legacies, some of considerable size, are administered by a community clearing house cooperating with the Van Wert Foundation. Within this framework function the Associated Char-

Van Wert County. The peony center of Ohio.

ities, peace and war chests, Boy Scouts, civic projects such as playgrounds, public health programs and the like. Income from the De Puy Fund of $25,000 has supplied indigent school children with books, clothing and glasses since 1874. The Brumback Public Library was the gift of John S. Brumback about 1890, in recognition of a library started years before by the women of Van Wert. It was the first county-wide public library in the United States, and special state laws had to be enacted to cover the county distribution feature.

The largest charity is the nationally famous Marsh Foundation School for orphaned and dependent children established in 1923 by George H. Marsh with a $5 million grant. The school occupies 1,400 acres on the edge of town. About 150 boys and girls live here and are educated from the first grade through high school. Trade and agricultural techniques are taught. Work is cooperative. Children are given an opportunity to earn money, and they leave, equipped for a trade or college and usually with savings accounts. The Marsh fortune stemmed from wood industries developed from the virgin forests of the region.

Van Wert has had few labor problems among its nearly twenty industries. A cheese factory, said to be the largest under one roof in the world, makes Liederkranz cheese. This was originated locally by a Swiss cheese maker who based his formula on an Old-World variety.

Southeast of Van Wert is Delphos, a city of 6,200 that lies in Van Wert and Allen Counties and spills over into Putnam. Streets have jogs, are of varying levels and form irregular corners at intersections, because the city grew in four sections, from four separate hamlets. The settlements expanded, and met. Citizens decided to combine the four and have one town. Delphos citizens say there is only one other place in the United States with this name, and that is a Kansas town christened for the Ohio city.

The most famous citizen is a toy designer by day and an astronomer by night. In his back yard observatory Leslie Peltier has discovered more than ten comets and several stars. He is a recognized authority on the performance of variable stars, and many heavenly bodies which he "found" have been named for him. His telescope was given him by Harvard University. Although he did not finish high school, honorary degrees from several universities have been conferred on him. His mother's gift of a book on the stars, and a fifteen-dollar telescope bought from money earned from farm chores started him at sixteen on his lifelong avocation.

ALLEN COUNTY, 1831

Named for a colonel who spent some time in this section during the War of 1812

ALLEN County had no town designated as a county seat. Settlers bought 160 acres of land in 1831 from the State for $200 and proceeded to lay out a city. The several names suggested for it were put in a hat. The one drawn was Lima, proposed by an early minister and congressman, Patrick Goode. The idea came to him because this Black Swamp area used great quantities of quinine or "Peruvian Bark" from Lima, Peru. Goode urged the South American pronunciation, "Leema." But a staunch Yankee countered: "It's spelled with an 'i' isn't it? Well, Lime-a is good enough for me." And "Lime-a" it's been ever since.

Allen County. Leslie Peltier of Delphos, well known amateur astronomer from Ohio.

A foreign visitor could find no better example than Lima of the quick evolution from American frontier to commercial metropolis. The town, on the edge of the swamp and in a primeval forest with no roads, found no takers for five-acre lots offered "with or without" credit. Today Lima is a city of over 50,000, second only to Toledo in Ohio's northwest. Its manufactures include locomotives, school buses, power shovels, steel, rubber products and cigars. A leading activity is processing farm products which range from sugar beets to dairy items.

Lima burst into fortune and fame accidentally. In 1885 Benjamin Faurot, influenced by the gas discovered the previous year in neighboring Findlay, decided to dig for gas for his paper mill. He struck a rich vein of oil, a fever of speculation hit and the public square, once a militia parade ground, bloomed with oil derricks. Lima had "the greatest oil fields known on the globe with a future beyond comprehension." By 1900 the oil tapered off. But Lima avoided the collapse that so often followed similar sudden expansions. The city maintains a key position in the industry with refineries, and as a center of pipe lines carrying millions of barrels of oil through here from fields in Texas and Oklahoma to Toledo, Cleveland, Chicago and other points.

Lima's Locomotive Works, covering many acres, and one of the largest plants of its kind in the world, manufactures all kinds of railroad engines. This city also takes pride in its past, and the Allen County Historical Museum is well worth a visit.

A few miles beyond Lima on the Auglaize River was Fort Amanda, now a pleasant park. Flatboats, built here when the river was a more vigorous stream, were used to transport men and supplies to Lake Erie under orders from Commodore Oliver Perry.

North of Lima is the Lima State Hospital for the Criminally Insane, a series of connected rectangular buildings with a single entrance, the whole resembling a fortress. About 1,000 acres of grounds surround it, and it is one of the biggest institutions of the kind in the world.

Bluffton was settled about the same time as Lima, by Swiss Mennonites who founded Bluffton College in 1900.

PAULDING COUNTY, 1839

Named for John Paulding, one of the captors of Major John André during the Revolutionary War

"No Compromise. The Reservoir Must Go." The message was crudely lettered on homemade banners waved aloft by 300 masked men. The reservoir of the abandoned Wabash-Erie canal covered 2,000 acres of good farm land near Antwerp, and had become a mosquito-infested swamp, a breeding ground for malaria. Citizens for years had tried without success to have the state drain it. One April night in 1887 they took matters in their own hands, and thereby hangs the tale of the most exciting event in Paulding County history. Residents along the canal were warned to

Paulding County. Six Mile Lagoon in the Auglaize River.

leave. A few hours later a terrific explosion cut into the quiet, lighting the sky with a glare seen for miles. With a mighty rush the water poured out. Horses caught in its path swam knee-deep in the current. Governor John B. Foraker ordered a company of militia from Toledo to Antwerp. The troops mounted guns along the canal and stood guard. The next night more masked dynamiters, appearing as if from no-where, swarmed over the embankment. The captain hastily pulled his soldiers away, and another charge let go, releasing all the water this time. The rioters rushed off, stopped a passing train and were whisked into Indiana, throwing passengers into a panic with their masks and guns. One of their number was arrested and taken to Paulding, the county seat. But he was almost immediately released. A state investi-gator, arriving in Antwerp a few days later, was met by a muttering mob. When they waved a rope and noose before him, he left at once. Governor Foraker visited the county later and was at pains to shake hands publicly with the leader of the "insurrection." The Dynamiters of Antwerp have gone down in county annals as heroes. Where the offending reservoir once was is now fine farm land.

Paulding County and the other counties in the northwest corner of the state were formed from Indian Territory about 1820. But they were settled much later because of the Black Swamp. This was a wasteland of bog and marsh extending southwest from Wood County into Indiana and north into Michigan. The Miami-Erie Canal and the Wabash-Erie from Indiana join in northern Paulding County; they were pushed through in the 1840s and helped open the country. But the real period of development was not until the 1870s and 1880s when the gigantic task of drainage was begun. More than 5,000 miles of ditches, main and subsidiary channels, were cut through this part of Ohio. The earth, freed from the grip of water, proved to be rich land for grain and grass crops, and of late years for sugar beets, tomatoes and cucumbers.

The early 1900s brought small industries that have expanded steadily in the last decade. There are few large towns. Paulding, a village of 2,400, the largest in the county, is a pleasant rural trading center with a leading factory making break linings. The county seat was first at Charloe, a hamlet named for an Indian chief.

PUTNAM COUNTY, 1820

Named for General Israel Putnam, veteran of the Indian and Revolutionary Wars, and cousin of General Rufus Putnam's father

SUGAR beets, tomatoes, corn, alfalfa—thousands of acres of each—stretch to the horizon from practically every point in Putnam County. And in the little towns and villages busy factories refine the beets into sugar, can the tomatoes or make them into soup and ketchup, and dehydrate the alfalfa. Ottawa, the center of all this and the county seat, has had growing pains the last few years. Along with food processing, it has new factories making television tubes and all-weather windows. Bond issues were passed in 1952 for new schools, the water supply was increased and a municipal

Putnam County. Spanish-Texan migrant workers who pick sugar beets, cherries and other crops in northwestern Ohio during the summer.

memorial park is under construction for community recreation needs. The progressive village of 3,200 is the largest in the county. It takes its name from Tawa Town, an ancient Indian village located for years on the site. French missionaries visited it many years before white traders or frontiersmen touched this area. A number of Indians remained here long after the main tribe moved west, living peaceably with white settlers. Germans, Swiss and Alsatians were among the early settlers. Citizens in Glandorf, near Ottawa, are largely of German Catholic descent. Pandora, to the southeast, was settled by Swiss Mennonites. This village, like Columbus Grove and Leipsic, are centers of tomato-growing and have tomato-canning factories.

Until Civil War times the county seat was at Kalida on the Ottawa River. The name Kalida was from the Greek word *kalos,* meaning "beautiful." In frontier times the river was referred to as Hog Creek because often hogs were drowned in the stream while being driven to supply the British at Fort Miami with pork.

The tiny village of Fort Jennings on the Auglaize River takes its name from the fort built by order of General William Henry Harrison who left Colonel William Jennings in charge of it.

DEFIANCE COUNTY, 1845

Named for Fort Defiance

"I DEFY the British, the Indians and all the devils in Hell to take this place." General Anthony Wayne could be forgiven for the swaggering boast. The fort he was building surely looked impregnable, commanding the point where the Maumee and the Auglaize rivers meet. "I'll call it Fort Defiance," added the general, strutting along the stockade, alert to every detail of the construction. He arrived in August 1794, probably expecting to engage the Indians at this place. Various tribes had lived along the two rivers for years. They were startled to have a white army penetrate this far, and many fled. So it was November when Wayne finally caught up with them and defeated them at Fallen Timbers, along the Maumee, a good many miles to the north.

If this confluence of the rivers was a good site for a fort, it was also a promising spot for a city. Defiance, taking its name from the fort, was the first town settled in the northwest corner of Ohio. For years government affairs for the surrounding counties were conducted from a stone courthouse here. In 1840 Defiance County was laid out between Williams and Paulding. This broke the original map plan in which Williams, Paulding and Van Wert, named for the three captors of Major André, were to join each other.

Defiance, now a busy city of 12,000, has made the most of its heritage. It boomed when the Miami-Erie and Indiana's Wabash canal met here. Around the old canal bed is Defiance State Park, and beyond, at the dam which controlled canal waters, is Independence Dam State Park. Independence was once a trade rival of Defiance, but there is little left of the village today. Wayne's old fort site is marked off as Defiance City Park.

In the northwest section of the city is the attractive wooded campus of Defiance College, a small co-educational institution. It was started as Defiance Female Seminary in 1850, the year which marked the beginning of so many Ohio colleges.

It is difficult for today's citizens to reconstruct the sight which greeted that early visitor, the confident Wayne. He found an imposing

236

Defiance County. Fort Defiance, built by General Anthony Wayne in 1794.

cluster of Indian tepees, crude bark huts and council houses. Defiance was old even then. Here tribal chiefs from Canada, the far west and the south had met for generations. The many tributaries of the Maumee and the Auglaize, then navigable for great distances, were convenient water highways. French traders and missionaries arrived thirty years before Wayne and gave the name Au Glaize to the river. Moravian Indian converts settled here after the Gnadenhutten massacre.

This was the homeland of Pontiac, born about 1720, and considered by many as the greatest of all Ohio Indians. Though friendly to the French, he saw the westward infiltration of the English as a threat to his race, and organized tribes from the Mississippi to New York State. In what was known as Pontiac's Conspiracy, in the 1760s many British outposts were captured by his followers, who killed and spread terror wherever they went.

HENRY COUNTY, 1824

Named for Patrick Henry, Virginia statesman

FRENCH and Germans were the first to pioneer in Henry County, and a spirited contest developed

Henry County. Inspectors grading tomatoes at a cannery in Napoleon.

between the two groups over naming the county seat. Some favored Henry, the name of the county. But the French group won out with their choice for a name, Napoleon. It was a natural location for a city along a particularly beautiful stretch of the Maumee River, and Napoleon became a prosperous center. The farms, averaging well over 100 acres each, from the early days to the present produced fine grain crops. In recent years they have been given over to tomatoes in fields hundreds of acres in size. Tomatoes are processed in Napoleon in two canning factories, subsidiaries of nationally known food companies. The thrifty city of 5,400 is noted for its fine schools and numerous churches.

In the Maumee River near Napoleon is a little island, known as Girty's Island. According to local tradition it was the home of George Girty, one of the four brothers notorious in frontier times. Not far from today's Napoleon, George and his brother James had an Indian trading post. It was an excellent spot since the river offered ready transportation. George's island home became a stronghold and retreat for all four brothers.

Today's Route 24, which runs beside the river through Napoleon from Toledo to Fort Wayne, is called the Anthony Wayne Trail and follows Wayne's line of march through here.

In the northern part of Henry County around Ridgeville Corners, so many Germans took up land that this section often was referred to as the Hanover settlement.

WILLIAMS COUNTY, 1824

Named for David Williams, one of the three captors of Major John André

"HALT!" Three colonial militia-men ran out of the woods near New York City. It was a mild September day in 1780. They had been playing cards under the trees when the sound of a galloping horse alerted them. They drew their rifles and stopped the rider. Little did they know this act would link them forever with Ohio, of which they probably never had heard.

"What do you want?"

The horseman was annoyed. "Who are you anyway?"

"We're Americans," they chorused.

"Well, then, here's my pass from one of your generals." He showed them an official paper authorizing him to go through American lines to New York. It was signed by General Benedict Arnold. The soldiers knew about Arnold—everyone did—and of his defense of the Connecticut towns against the British, of his service under Washington. David Williams, the oldest of the trio—and he was not quite twenty-three—had been at the siege of Montreal when Arnold, though badly wounded, led the Americans' retreat that terrible winter of 1775. Last month, Williams reminded his companions, Arnold had been made commandant of the nearby fort, West Point. They could not know that Arnold, despite his fine record, was disgruntled over fancied slights by the military and had turned traitor.

The soldiers were Hudson River Dutchmen who spoke English with difficulty. They were young and unsure of themselves. The stranger was handsome, with a commanding way about him, and the clothes of a gentleman. A friend of General Arnold! They wished

Williams County. Bryan, county seat, is the home of the Fisher-Smith Archery Company.

they had not stopped him and were about to send him on, when they asked him some questions. He replied so oddly that they became suspicious and ordered him to dismount. He refused until they raised their muskets. They undressed him, finding nothing incriminating until they pulled off his fine leather boots. In both were wads of papers with detailed maps of West Point's layout.

"He's an English spy!" exclaimed Williams. The other two, John Paulding and Isaac Van Wart, were not convinced until their captive began offering them rewards if they would free him. Much excited now, they hunted up an officer and turned the man over to him. Then they learned he was Major John André, close associate of the British commander-in-chief, Sir Henry Clinton. The American officer notified Arnold of the capture, unaware it was Arnold's own plan for the betrayal of West Point to the British which André was carrying. Arnold, thus tipped off, escaped. The unfortunate André was hanged despite pleas to General Washington for his acquittal, not only from the British but from many sympathetic Americans as well. The three youths who captured the British major were rewarded with farms, annuities and medals by the government, and their names given to Ohio's three northwestern counties—Williams, Paulding and Van Wert (the spelling changed from Van Wart).

Williams County, tucked into Ohio's extreme northwest corner, with Michigan on its north and Indiana on its west, was one of the last sections in this state to be settled. The great problem was ridding the land of the endless giant trees which today would bring fortunes in lumber. Early county history abounds in tales of pioneers getting lost in the woods, often ·when within a few yards of their cabin homesteads. The forests were full of wild animals, and hunts went on that rivaled any in other parts of the state. In 1830, when Ohio had almost a million population, there were scarcely 1,000 persons in all Williams County.

Bryan, the county seat, was not selected until 1840. The site was donated by John Bryan, state auditor. Many French from the Detroit area, as well as Germans from the south, settled around here. It is a conservative pleasant city of 6,500, the largest in the county. It has a few industries, but its Main Street business is largely that of a trading center for the farms of the county.

FULTON COUNTY, 1850

Named for Robert Fulton, inventor and builder of the first commercially successful steamboat, the Clermont, 1807

In its four hundred years of living, the great Council Oak at Winameg has shaded Indians in the fury of war dances, and in the quiet of peace councils. Its topmost tips have been pierced by the agonized shrieks of white prisoners lashed to its trunk as practice targets for sharp-shooting Indian lads, and as victims of the fiendish tomahawk. The tree was already old in the days of Pontiac, two hundred years ago when the Potawatamie Indians met under its branches. When first settlers came into this part of Ohio, several years before the county was formed, the tree was pointed out proudly by Chief Winameg who lived here in a village named for

Fulton County. The largest plant in the world for making Chinese food products is at Archbold.

him, the largest Indian encampment in the northwest. The Ohio town carries the name still. An early settler's son, Colonel D. W. H. Howard, learned the Indian language from playing with the Indian children, and was appointed interpreter for this part of the country by President Jackson. Chief Winameg related to Colonel Howard more than once the doings under the tree, "our revenge for the many wrongs of the Palefaces to our people," he always added as his face darkened with anger. Howard recorded it all in his official papers, so the tree's history comes down to present-day Ohioans with the ring of authenticity. Colonel Howard and Chief Winameg both are buried near it.

Wauseon, twelve miles south of Winameg, was platted in the 1850s but did not become the county seat until 1870. In 1878 Barney Oldfield, pioneer auto racer, was born here. Wauseon's population is now 3,500, and it is the largest town in the county. It is on the old ridge which led south through Defiance and Van Wert, a well marked Indian route followed by Wayne in 1794. The trail went east to Delta, laid out in 1834 and the oldest town in the county. When the county was organized the seat of government was located temporarily at Wauseon until moved north to Ottokee, a village now of 100 population. Pioneers thought Ottokee had a future, for back in the 1820s the state built a turnpike through here. It went from the Western Reserve to the Maumee, and $20,000 was appropriated to pave it with the new macadam cement. The road was the chief immigrant and mail route for years, and a great boon to the frontier. But the courthouse at Ottokee burned, and the seat of government finally went to Wauseon.

Fulton County, tucked up next door to Michigan, opened slowly to settlement. The district is interspersed with many woodlots and small swales affording cover for wild life and game; the county is a hunters' haven. In a forest stretch, the Oak Openings, squirrel, pheasant and rabbit abound, but the favorite pastime is 'coon hunting. Harrison Lake, covering over 100 acres, and made by the Division of Wild Life in 1940, is a popular spot for picnicking. Another pretty body of water is the reservoir at Delta, well stocked with large-mouthed bass and bluegill. Because of the touch of the glacier, many plants grow here which are rare in other sections of Ohio. Fulton County is a hunting ground for the man with a gun and for the botanist.

At Archbold is an odd industry for Ohio, a plant making Chinese food products. This plant is claimed by its management to be the largest business of its kind in the world. The factory covers four and a half acres, employs between 200 and 300 persons. Celery, the biggest item processed, is received in carload lots and is mixed with other ingredients to make chop suey and chow mein products.

WOOD COUNTY, 1820

Named for Colonel Wood who helped build Fort Meigs

SCRAMBLING to the log and earth parapet of Fort Meigs, General William Henry Harrison waved his arms frantically to warn the Kentucky colonel, William Dudley, and his men of the danger. Dudley, mistaking the signals for encouragement, plunged on. Soon he and his 800 militia were ambushed by

British and Indians many times their number. Only 150 escaped. The wounded and captives, including Dudley, were systematically tortured by the Indians. The British general, Henry Proctor, looked on indifferently, but Tecumseh, leader of the Indians, rushed into the melee and stopped the carnage. When the news reached the fort, soldiers dashed out recklessly and attacked the nearest British battery. Its surprised gunners surrendered. The Indians, certain their luck had turned, ran off. Proctor, seeing his forces were completely demoralized, withdrew. The siege of Fort Meigs was lifted in May 1813. Its defenders became the heroes of the frontier. They halted the British invasion of northern Ohio. The fort, on the east bank of the Maumee River, was named for Return Jonathan Meigs, the Ohio governor at the time.

The site of this suffering and bloodshed is marked by a commemorative shaft set in the 50-acre Fort Meigs State Park. Dudley and his men are buried in a cemetery here. Close by, in Perrysburg, named for Oliver Hazard Perry, an imposing monument to the naval hero overlooks the Maumee. Perrysburg's handsome old houses under arching trees are rich in ancient legend. Some were taverns, patronized by stagecoaches plying between Buffalo and St. Louis.

Between Perrysburg and Toledo to the north is an exclusive residence district, with miles of walled estates. Perrysburg was the county seat until 1866 when Bowling Green usurped it. In 1914 a state normal school was opened; it became a college in 1929 and, by 1935, state-supported Bowling Green University.

Rural Wood County is one vast open space of straight-marked fields of soybeans, corn, alfalfa, oats, wheat, tomatoes, sugar beets; straight good roads; straight drainage ditches spread flatly for miles. Scattered houses rise large against the horizon and the numerous grain elevators loom like skyscrapers.

While New Rumley, Harrison County, receives much attention as the birthplace (1839) of the Indian fighter, General George Armstrong Custer, Ohio seems to have overlooked the fact that Wood County was also home to Custer. The family spent the Civil War years on a farm near Tontagony, northwest of Bowling Green. The village, named for an Indian chief, is shortened locally to To'gany. A faded sign tacked to a tree proclaims a tumble-down cabin, now a

Wood County. The Oliver Hazard Perry Monument in Perrysburg, overlooking the Maumee River.

farm workshop, as the "Custar" homestead. The "a" is Wood County spelling for the name and occurs in the nearby village of Custar, presumably christened for the general. The general's father, Emmanuel Custer, paid $2,000 for the Tontagony farm when he moved from New Rumley in 1861. That year his son was graduated from West Point and went immediately into service. He rose from second lieutenant to captain and became a general at twenty-three, one of the youngest in the army. He was in action during the whole of the war. He spent his furloughs in Tontagony. Residents point out the spot near the depot where the general, when returning to the front, tied his horse, leaving it to be taken back to the farm by his brothers. A brother of Custer, Tom, later a colonel, enlisted in the war from To'gany. He, another brother, a brother-in-law and a nephew all were killed with Custer in 1876 at the Battle of the Little Big Horn in Wyoming, the country's last Indian foray. Another brother, Nevin, had a farm on the edge of Tontagony. His son, Armstrong, received his uncle's saddle following the western battle, and for years, until it was lost, it was a prized village relic. Custer's parents left Tontagony at the end of the Civil War for Monroe, Michigan, where the general's beloved half-sister, Lydia, lived and where Custer had attended an academy in preparation for West Point.

LUCAS COUNTY, 1835

Named for Robert Lucas, then governor of Ohio

IN THE eerie stillness of one o'clock in the morning three paunchy Ohio judges, guarded by a detachment of cavalry, rode cautiously into Toledo. While their escorts reined to attention outside, the judges dismounted and stealthily entered a schoolhouse. By the wavering light of a couple of tallow dips, they held court, then blew out their candles and hurriedly rode off. In their haste, the top hat of one was brushed off by a tree twig. A soldier bravely went back and picked it up. Hidden in its lining was an important document, the official record of the meeting. The midnight ride of the judges thwarted the Michigan militia who were standing in readiness to swoop down on Toledo and stop the court session, which they had expected would be held later that day at the usual hour. It was an episode in the comic-opera Michigan-Toledo boundary "war" of 1835 in which Michigan claimed a strip of Ohio that included Toledo. There was considerable parading back and forth of both states' militia. However, the action of Ohio's governor, Robert Lucas, in creating Lucas County out of Wood County, and President Jackson's gift of Wisconsin Territory's upper peninsula to Michigan, settled the dispute before any blood was shed.

At this time Toledo was a very young city, born two years before by the consolidation of two towns, Vistula and Port Lawrence, and given its pleasant Spanish name because no other Ohio town was so called. Bogged down by panic and a summer of terrible drought in the late 1830s, Toledo did not get under way until the 1840s brought the Wabash-Erie Canal from Indiana and the Miami-Erie as a trade link with southern Ohio. About this time the stout oak tracks of one of the country's pioneer railroads, the Kalamazoo-Erie, were laid from Adrian, Michigan, to Toledo; the first cars were pulled by horses. The

Lucas County. Toledo as seen from the Anthony Wayne Parkway bridge.

fine harbor had attracted lake trade since the seventeenth century when French voyagers unfurled their sails at the mouth of the Maumee; it was to become an important factor in the growth of the modern Toledo.

Today this city of over 300,000, the county seat, is the greatest coal shipping port in the world, and one of the most important Great Lakes grain and ore ports. The discovery of natural gas in the 1880s lured a glass manufacturer, Edward Libbey, from Cambridge, Massachusetts. He hired Michael Owens, a glass blower from Wheeling, as superintendent of his plant. Ten years later Edward Ford developed the town of Rossford below Toledo, and established there one of the nation's largest plate glass factories. By mid-nineteenth century Toledo was the "glass capital" of the world. Pioneer bicycle and wagon industries led to auto parts and accessories. Toledo is also a nationally important petroleum refining center. The Toledo Museum of Art is one of the six largest in the United States with the world's finest glass collection. The University of Toledo, a municipal university, uses as an emblem the coat of arms of Spain's Isabella and Ferdinand. A further reminder of the city's Spanish name is the Cathedral of Toledo, built in the architectural style of the churches of Spain.

Toledo and the fertile Maumee Valley fanning from it are historic lands, prized and long fought over by Indians, French, British and Americans. Anthony Wayne's confident footsteps echo everywhere: the site of Fort Industry, within the city limits, built by him as an impudent warning to the nearby British Fort Miami; the $3 million Anthony Wayne suspension bridge across the river.

Below Toledo is the charming little town of Maumee, cherishing its old memories and old houses. It looks across the broad river, grown peaceful now after so much warfare, to the looming towers and tree-tops of Perrysburg on the opposite bank. At Maumee occurred the Battle of Fallen Timbers, which lasted less than an hour and ended twenty years of Indian menace. The field on that November day in 1794 was a tangle of tornado-strewn trees, which gave the important engagement its name. It is a state park now, with a statue showing Wayne between a tough militia man and an Indian holding a peace pipe.

The Rock, in the river at Waterville, was christened Roche de Boeuf by the French 250 years ago, before it had broken away from the shore. For generations it has been Waterville's play spot. Waterville was a stopover for stagecoach passengers, who put up at a big inn which is still standing. In canal days Waterville's long wharf was a crowded shipping point for grain.

OHIO COLLEGES AND UNIVERSITIES

Bowling Green State University, Bowling Green; 1914; coed.; small-town envir.; undergrad. & grad.

Central State College, Wilberforce; 1947; coed.; small-town envir.; undergrad., originally incorporated as part of Wilberforce University (1887).

Kent State University, Kent; 1910; coed.; small-town envir.; undergrad. & grad.

Miami University, Oxford; 1809; coed.; small-town envir.; undergrad. & grad.

Ohio State University, Columbus; 1873; coed.; urban envir.; undergrad., grad. & prof.

Ohio University, Athens; 1804; coed.; small-town envir.; undergrad. & grad.

Akron, University of, Akron; 1870; coed.; urban envir.; undergrad. & grad.

Cincinnati, University of, Cincinnati; 1819; coed.; urban envir.; undergrad., grad. & prof.

Toledo, University of, Toledo; 1872; coed.; urban envir.; undergrad. & grad.

Antioch College, Yellow Springs; 1853; coed.; small-town envir.; co-operative work-and-study plan; undergrad.

Ashland College, Ashland; 1878; coed.; small-town envir.; undergrad.

Baldwin-Wallace College, Berea; 1845; coed.; small-town envir.; undergrad.

Bluffton College, Bluffton, 1900; coed.; small-town envir.; undergrad.

Capital University, Columbus; 1850; coed.; urban envir.; undergrad.

Case Institute of Technology, Cleveland; 1881; men; urban envir.; undergrad. & grad.

Cedarville College, Cedarville; 1894; coed.; small-town envir.; undergrad. & grad.

Dayton, University of, Dayton; 1850; coed.; urban envir.; undergrad. & grad.

Defiance College, Defiance; 1850; coèd.; small-town envir.; undergrad.

Denison University, Granville; 1831; coed.; small-town envir.; undergrad.

Fenn College, Cleveland; 1923; coed.; urban envir.; undergrad.

Findlay College, Findlay; 1884; coed.; small-town envir.; undergrad.

Heidelberg College, Tiffin; 1850; coed.; small-town envir.; undergrad.

Hiram College, Hiram; 1850; coed.; rural envir.; undergrad.

John Carroll University, University Heights (Cleveland); 1886; men, partly coed.; urban envir.; undergrad. & grad.

Kenyon College, Gambier; 1824; men; rural envir.; undergrad.

Lake Erie College, Painesville; 1859; women; small-town envir.; undergrad.

Marietta College, Marietta, 1835; coed.; small-town envir.; undergrad. & grad.-

Mary Manse College, Toledo; 1922; women; urban envir.; undergrad.

Mount Saint Joseph-on-the-Ohio, College of, Mount Saint Joseph (Cincinnati); 1920; women; urban envir.; undergrad.

Mount Union College, Alliance; 1846; coed.; small-town envir.; undergrad.

Muskingum College, New Concord; 1837; coed.; small-town envir.; undergrad.

Notre Dame College, South Euclid (Cleveland); 1922; women; urban envir.; undergrad.

Oberlin College, Oberlin; 1833; coed.; small-town envir.; undergrad. & grad.

Ohio Northern University, Ada; 1871; coed.; small-town envir.; undergrad.

Ohio Wesleyan University, Delaware; 1842; coed.; small-town envir.; undergrad. & grad.

Otterbein College, Westerville; 1847; coed.; small-town envir.; undergrad.

Our Lady of Cincinnati College, Cincinnati; 1935; women; urban envir.; undergrad.

Rio Grande College, Rio Grande; 1876; coed.; rural envir.; undergrad.

Saint John College, Cleveland; 1928; women; urban envir.; teaching & nursing; undergrad.

Saint Mary of the Springs College, Columbus; 1911; women; urban envir.; undergrad.

Ursuline College for Women, Cleveland; 1871; women; urban envir.; undergrad.

Western College for Women, Oxford; 1853; women; small-town envir.; undergrad.

Western Reserve University, Cleveland; 1826; coed.; urban envir.; undergrad., grad. & prof.

Wilberforce University, Wilberforce; 1856; predominantly Negro, coed.; small-town envir.; undergrad.

Wilmington College, Wilmington; 1863; coed.; small-town envir.; undergrad.

Wittenberg College, Springfield; 1845; coed.; urban envir.; undergrad.

Wooster, College of, Wooster; 1870; coed.; small-town envir.; undergrad.

Xavier University, Cincinnati; 1831; men, partly coed.; urban envir.; undergrad. & grad.

Youngstown College, Youngstown; 1908; coed.; urban envir.; undergrad.

BIBLIOGRAPHY

ALLEN, HUGH: *Rubber's Home Town.* New York: Stratford House, 1949.
A Memoir of Rev. Joseph Badger. Sawyer, Ingersoll and Company, 1851.

BACON, THEODORE: *Delia Bacon.* New York: Houghton, Mifflin and Company, 1888.
BAKER, NINA BROWN: *Cyclone in Calico.* Boston: Little, Brown and Company, 1952.
BENNETT, MARTHA TRIMBLE: *Ohio's First Capital.* An outline history of Chillicothe and Ross County.
BENTON, ELBERT JAY: *Cultural Story of an American City, Cleveland.* Cleveland: Western Reserve Historical Society, 1943.
BOWMAN, DAVID W.: *Pathways of Progress.* New York: American Book Company, 1943.
BRODIE, FAWN M.: *No Man Knows My History* (Life of Joseph Smith). New York, 1945.
BROWN, HALLIE Q., compiler and editor: *Pen Pictures of Pioneers of Wilberforce.* The Aldine Publishing Company, 1937.

CHASE, JULIA A.: *Mary A. Bickerdyke, "Mother."* Journal Publishing House, 1896.
CROUSE, DAVID: *The Ohio Gateway.* New York: Charles Scribner's Sons.

DICKENS, CHARLES: *American Notes.* John W. Lovell Company.
DOWNES, RANDOLPH CHANDLER: *Ohio Historical Collections, Frontier Ohio, 1788–1803.* Ohio State Archaeological and Historical Society, 1935.

EDDY, MARY O: *Ballads and Songs from Ohio.* J. J. Augustin Publisher, 1939.

FAUSET, ARTHUR HUFF: *Sojourner Truth.* The University of North Carolina Press, 1944.
FINN, CHESTER E.: *The Ohio Canals: Public Enterprise on the Frontier.* Reprint from Ohio State Archaeological and Historical Quarterly, March 1942.
FRARY, I. T.: *Early Homes of Ohio.* Garrett and Massie, Inc., 1936.
———: *Ohio in Homespun and Calico.* Garrett and Massie, Inc., 1942.

GREEN, JAMES A.: *William Henry Harrison, His Life and Times.* Garrett and Massie, Inc., 1941.

Hanna, Book of Benjamin. Privately printed in Cleveland, 1938.

HARLOW, ALVIN: *The Serene Cincinnatians.* New York: E. P. Dutton and Company, Inc., 1950.

HATCHER, HARLAN: *The Western Reserve.* Indianapolis: The Bobbs-Merrill Company, 1949.

HAVIGHURST, WALTER: *Land of Promise.* New York: The Macmillan Company, 1946.

HEALD, EDWARD THORNTON: *Bezaleel Wells.* The Stark County Historical Society, 1948.

————: *The Stark County Story,* 2 vols. The Stark County Historical Society, 1949.

History of Ashtabula County. William Bros., 1878.

HOWE, HENRY: *Historical Collections of Ohio,* 1846–1886. C. J. Krehbiel and Company, 1888.

LEWIS, LLOYD: *Sherman, Fighting Prophet.* New York: Harcourt, Brace and Company, 1932.

LEWIS, W. G. W.: *Biography of Samuel Lewis.* The Methodist Book Concern, 1857.

MORGAN, VIOLET: *Folklore of Highland County.* The Greenfield Printing and Publishing Company, 1946.

NOTESTEIN, LUCY LILIAN: *Wooster of the Middle West.* New Haven: Yale University Press, for the College of Wooster, 1937.

Ohio Guide, The. Oxford University Press, 1943.

Ohio, An Empire within an Empire. Ohio Development and Publicity Commission, 2nd Edition, 1951.

Ohio Archaeological and Historical Society Publications. Fred J. Heer, 1915.

OSBURN, MARY HUBBELL: *Ohio Composers and Musical Authors.* Fred J. Heer, 1942.

PETERS, WILLIAM E.: *Ohio Lands and Their History.* Athens, Ohio: W. E. Peters, 1930.

PIERCY, CAROLINE B.: *The Valley of God's Pleasure.* Stratford House, 1951.

Record of Hon. C. L. Vallandigham, The. J. Walter and Company, 1836.

REDPATH, JAMES: *The Public Life of Capt. John Brown.* Thayer and Eldridge, 1860.

ROSE, WILLIAM GANSON: *Cleveland: The Making of a City.* Cleveland: The World Publishing Company, 1950.

ROSEBOOM, EUGENE HOLLOWAY AND WEISENBURGER, FRANCIS PHELPS: *History of Ohio.* New York: Prentice-Hall, Inc., 1934.

SAFFORD, WILLIAM H.: *The Blennerhassett Papers*. Moore, Wilstach, Keys and Company, 1861.

SCHNEIDER, NORRIS F.: *Y-Bridge City*. Cleveland: The World Publishing Company, 1950.

SIBLEY, WILLIAM G.: *The French Five Hundred*. Gallia County Historical Society, 1933.

SIEBERT, WILBUR HENRY: *The Mysteries of Ohio's Underground Railroads*. Long's College Book Company, 1951.

SIEDEL, FRANK: *The Ohio Story*. Cleveland: The World Publishing Company, 1950.

SMITH, C. HENRY: *The Story of the Mennonites*. Mennonite Book Concern, 1941.

SMITH, JOSEPH, JR., translator: *The Book of Mormon*. Board of Publication of the Reorganized Church of Jesus Christ of Latter Day Saints, 1946.

SWARTHWOUT, ANNIE FERN: *Missie, The Life and Times of Annie Oakley*. The Brown Publishing Company, 1947.

THARP, LOUISE HALL: *The Peabody Sisters of Salem*. Boston: Little, Brown and Company, 1950.

TROLLOPE, FRANCIS: *Domestic Manners of the Americans*. New York: Alfred A. Knopf, Inc., 1949.

UPTON, HARRIET TAYLOR: *Random Collections*.

WAITE, FREDERICK CLAYTON: *Western Reserve University, The Hudson Era*. Cleveland: Western Reserve University Press, 1943.

WHITE, RUTH YOUNG, editor: *We, Too, Built Columbus*. Stoneman Press, 1936.

WILCOX, FRANK: *Ohio Indian Trails*. The Gates Press, 1933.

WILSON, FORREST: *Crusader in Crinoline* (Life of Harriet Beecher Stowe). Philadelphia: J. B. Lippincott Company, 1941.

WILSON, FRASER E.: *Around the Council Fire*.

———: *Arthur St. Clair*. Garrett and Massie, 1941.

WITTKE, CARL, editor: *History of the State of Ohio*, 6 vols. The Ohio State Archaeological and Historical Society, 1944.

WOLFE, WILLIAM G.: *Stories of Guernsey County*. Published by the author, 1943.

Numerous county histories, publications of the Ohio Chamber of Commerce and of chambers in many Ohio cities; Western Reserve Historical Society, Cleveland; *The Ohio Daily Industrial Trade News*, and many documents, diaries and letters in private hands throughout the state.

INDEX

Ada, 147
Adams County, 175–177
Adena, 177
Adventure Galley, 17
Akron, 51, 52, 54, 55
Albi Cottage, 98
Allen County, 230–232
Allen County Historical Museum, 232
Allen, Judge Florence E., 42
Allger, General Russell A., 57
Alliance, 67, 68
Alum Creek, 78
American Rolling Mills Company, 203
American Shipbuilding Company, 58
Amesville, 21
Amherst, 59
Amish, 43, 72, 82–85
Amos, General James O., 226
Anderson, Sherwood, 84, 139
André, Major John, 232, 236, 239–241
Anthony Wayne Country, 194
Antioch College, 211, 212
Anti-Saloon League, 127
Antwerp, 233
Appleseed, Johnny (John Chapman), 72, 75
Archbold, 243
Archbold, John D., 95
Arkites, 48
Arnold, General Benedict, 239, 240
Ash Cave, 129
Ashland, 72, 74
Ashland College, 72, 74
Ashland County, 30, 72–74
Ashtabula, 32, 34, 47
Ashtabula County, 30–31
Athens, 16, 20
Athens County, 20
Atwater, Caleb, 183
Atwater Congregational Church, 45–46
Auglaize County, 226–228
Aultman, 55
Aurora, 45
Austin, Mrs. Eliphalet, 32
Austinburg, 32
Ava, 111, 112

Bacon, Reverend David, 54
Bacon, Delia, 54
Badger, Reverend Joseph, 37
Baldwin, Michael, 178
Baldwin-Wallace College, 51
Ball, Ernest, 143

Barber, Ohio Columbus (Match King), 54
Barlow, Joel, 27
Barnesville, 102
Barnum, Eli, 35
Barnum, P. T., 36, 57
Batavia, 201
Bates, Captain M. V. and Mrs., 56
Beard, Dan, 40
Beecher, Harriet (Mrs. Stowe), 170, 171
Beecher, Lyman, 170, 171, 196
Bellaire, 103
Bellaire, Zanesville & Western Railroad, 105
Bellefontaine, 157
Belmont County, 94, 101–103
Benedict, Platt, 62
Bennett, James, 64
Berea, 51
Berlin, 85
Beveridge, Albert J., 170
Bexley Hall, 80
Bexley, Lord, 80
Bickerdyke, Mary Ann Ball, 80–82
Bienville, Celeron de, 187–189
Bimeler, Joseph, 92
Birch, Hugh, 213
Birchard Public Library, 138
Birchard, Sardis, 123, 138
Black River, 57
Black Swamp, 140, 230, 234
Blanchard River, 143
Blennerhassett, Harman, 18, 19
Blennerhassett Island, 18
Blooming Grove, 153
Bluffton, 232
Bluffton College, 232
Bolton, Frances P., 44
Boone, Daniel, 147
Borglum, Gutzon, 19
Boston, 15
Bouquet, Colonel Henry, 88
Bowling Green, 244
Bowling Green University, 244
Bradley, Captain Alva, 48
Brady Lake, 44
Brady's Leap, 44
Brady, Sam, 44
Brant, Chief, 116–117
Brecksville, 51
Brier Hill Furnaces, 37
Bristolville, 37
Brock, 219